Building
A
Legacy of Love

Dedication

Dedicated to our Blessed Mother in Heaven and in special recognition to the mothers in our midst who live as God calls them to live, and to those unsung and unknown birthmothers who responded in faith like Moses' mother, choosing adoption in order that their little ones may have life.

Published by: The Riehle Foundation

Additional copies of this book may be acquired by contacting:

For individuals: The Riehle Foundation
                    P.O. Box 7
                    Milford, Ohio 45150-0007
                    USA
                    Phone: 1-513-576-0032
                    Fax: 1-513-576-0022

For book stores: Faith Publishing Company
                    P.O. Box 237
                    Milford, Ohio 45150-0237
                    USA
                    Phone: 1-513-576-6400
                    Fax: 1-513-576-0022

Front cover illustration: Ann McCullough

Foreword

Building A Legacy of Love is an excellent book which runs the gamut of issues that face most Christian couples in today's society. Yet Mary Ann Kuharski's approach is mixed with common sense, humor, and is always faith filled! She is a traditional Catholic mother who is forever optimistic about the power of prayer and the promise of Sanctifying Grace that God offers to faithful parents.

Readers of Mary Ann's first book *Raising Catholic Children*, were introduced to the Kuharski family of 13 children, six of whom are adopted and of "special needs." A pro-life activist and adoption advocate, Mary Ann shared her wealth of experiences about teaching children to pray, resolving sibling rivalry, taking toddlers to church and easing the challenges of motherhood. In her second book *Parenting With Prayer*, Mary Ann focuses on a parent's most important task: forming the spiritual life of children. Using stories and anecdotes, this helpful book addresses everything from Sacraments and Saints to sin.

Building A Legacy of Love addresses many issues most parents face today, such as "discipline," "TV watching," "manners," "self-control," "building self-esteem," and most importantly, "faith building." Mary Ann offers practical advice regarding growing childrens involvement in "sports," as well as timely topics on "dating," "marriage," the "single life," and "vocations." These are intertwined with such concerns as care of extended family members and living out our Christian witness through everyday practices such as family dinnertime and family prayer.

Mary Ann and her husband John, have as their highest priority, more than building trust, confidence and self-esteem in their children. Their goal is to build a foundation in their young that will bring them happiness and peace of mind—here and in the hereafter. Make no mistake, the Kuharski's are Heaven bound, and Mary Ann's writings continue to encourage readers in the same direction.

Paul V. Dudley,
Bishop of the Diocese of Sioux Falls (retired)

Table of Contents

Introduction

To the outside world, our task as parents may not appear noble or noteworthy, but when we live our lives as God calls us to live, right where we are stationed, we are pleasing God and doing His Will. Even when that means doing dishes at the kitchen sink, folding another endless pile of clothes, or playing taxi for our kids events.

That's what I love about God. He sees each of us, and the work we do in His name, as important in helping to build up The Mystical Body of Christ. And, as the mother of thirteen children, ages 8 to 28, I relate best to "kitchen sink" and "laundry duty."

As for our own "mystical" body, let me admit that Johnny and I cheated a bit on bringing our family together. You see, seven of our children came from "Mom's tummy," as the kids would say, and "six came by airplane or adoption."

We are a colorful crew with many of our "tummy" kids resembling my fair-skinned Polish husband, John. He's also the more tranquil, with a mild, easy-going nature that almost drives me to despair at times. I'm the more compulsive "Type A-personality" and if that weren't enough, my Italian background should fill in the rest of the picture.

Our adopted crew rounds out our curves as they came at varied ages and stages from countries near and far, including Vietnam, the Philippines, East India, and two from the U.S., one Mexican American and one Black American.

Needless to say, parenting this large and multi-faceted family has not been predictable or problem-free, but it has brought us closer as a couple than we ever dreamed possible, and added more love than any family deserves to have—proving that God is never outdone in generosity.

Pope John Paul II says families are the "Domestic Church" because the seeds of faith begin in the home with us.

That's a pretty scary thought to know that we are the primary educators, the *First Missionaries*, to our children. Until we remember that we have help. And that's just what God offers through faith and the special grace that comes through the Sacrament of Matrimony and all the other Sacraments.

Jesus said, *"You are the Light of the World. A city set on a hill cannot be hidden. Men do not light a lamp and then put it under a bushel basket. They set it on a stand where it gives light to all in the house. In the same way, your light must shine before men so that they may see goodness in your acts and give praise to your Heavenly Father."* (*Matthew* 5:14-17).

Christ could have said "all in the community," or "all in the Congress" but he didn't. He said our light must shine for "all in the house." (Sometimes community or Congress might seem easier.) But he promised to be with us always and to give us the grace needed to fulfill our mission. All we need do is *ask!*

As parents, we have a special assignment: to create a climate of good, a "Civilization of Love," as Pope John Paul II says. When we work to make our home a haven of faith-filled love, it will radiate like light to everyone around us!

Mother Teresa of Calcutta said it best: "It is easy to love people far away. It is not always easy to love those close to us. It is easier to give a cup of water to relieve hunger than to relieve the loneliness and pain of someone unloved in our own home. Bring love into your home for this is where our love for each other must start."

Much like the passing down of family traditions and recipes, so too, our faith traditions should be handed down to our children and grandchildren, wrapped warmly and securely in a lifetime of love.

Most women enjoy exchanging recipes. Women of faith are no different. Yet our goal is more than the physical nourishment of our children. We want to know the ingredients that will help our kids reach that ultimate and final goal—eternal happiness in heaven. That's what Christian parenting is really all about!

This little book is part of my personal story. It offers some of my own and others time-tested ingredients in raising Christian children and helping to create that *"Civilization of love."*

I've also tossed in some favorite Kuharski family recipes, nothing gourmet or too fancy, mind you. After all, I'm talking "tight budget," not to mention a host of average eaters (spelled "p i c k y ") who can deflate an ego and ruin a creative cook's concoction by spooning out at sight, even a morsel of chopped celery, cooked cauliflower, camouflaged mushroom, sautéed onion, diced tomato, or heaven forbid, lima bean!

You may have met them before in my previous books *Raising Catholic Children* and *Parenting with Prayer*, (Our Sunday Visitor Press), but let me re-introduce my own *Building A Legacy of Love.*

John—my wonderful husband of 30 years, claims he still doesn't understand me and hasn't yet reached his goal of "trying to slow me down and *reform* me." "Isn't that nice, Honey." I tell him. "Marriage is another of God's mysteries! All you have to do is just keep loving me." And he does!

Our Kuharski Crew:

Chrissy—(29, "tummy") is married to her own Prince Charming, Andy Klaesges. They now have three beautiful little girls: Elizabeth (3), and Ann Marie (18 months) and Carolyn (1 month).

Tim—(27, "tummy") is married to Tina, the girl of his dreams, and answer to our prayers.

Charlie—(27, adopted, Vietnamese Black) recently served four years in the United States Air Force and now works in Colorado as an electrical engineer.

Tina—(26, adopted, Philippines) now works as a nurse at a Minneapolis hospital.

Tony—(24, adopted, Vietnamese) is serving in the Infantry with the United States Army.

Vincent—(26, adopted, East India) works in the Twin Cities area.

Theresa—(22, adopted Black American) lives in Red Wing, Minnesota.

<u>Still living at home are:</u>

Mary Elizabeth—(18, "tummy") is a freshman in college. She's our "casual" one who (hates cleaning) loves cooking, shopping at secondhand thrift stores, and experimenting with hair color!

Angela (Angie)—(16, "tummy") a sophomore at a Catholic High School, she's nicknamed "little Mary" by fellow students and helps pay for tuition (as did her sisters and brothers before her) by working at a local donut shop. She still has time for sports, babysitting, cruising the Malls, and bumming with her sisters.

Karen (Kari)—(15, "tummy") following the leaders, Kari, known by friends as "Ku Bear," is a freshman in high school. She manages to sandwich sports, a weekly paper route (tuition), babysitting, and piano. She's our poet, writer, and "neat nick"! These three girls are the best of buddies!

Michael—(13, "tummy") a seventh-grader, is now the oldest Kuharski at St. Charles Borromeo School. He's so happy to finally reach the top of at least one "heap"! Michael *lives* baseball and in between his weekly paper route (tuition), soccer, baseball, and basketball, he collects and trades baseball cards. His collection now numbers over 5000!

Dominic—(11, adopted, Mexican American) is in the 5th grade at St. Charles. Dommie loves working with his hands, just so long as they're wrapped around a remote control, computer game, or anything but work. There's potential here and we've channeled it toward school work, outdoor play and most recently trumpet lessons (I'm excited). He's all boy!

Joseph—(8, "tummy") God's "encore," is in the 3rd grade at St. Charles. While others our age may be talking condos in the south or retirement, Joseph keeps us thinking young, as we run through one more Kindergarten, First Communion, simple reader, two wheel trainer, Tooth Fairy visit, and all the rest. God is so good!

From our house to yours, and as people of faith headed for that ultimate goal, Heaven, may God bless you and your family, as you work to create your own "legacy of love."

CHAPTER 1

Nearness Is Reassuring To Big And Little People

"The Lord is my light and my salvation; whom should I fear? The Lord is the strength of my life; of whom shall I be afraid?" (*Psalm* 27:1).

I remember the time I convinced Johnny to buy an inexpensive area rug for the basement. Nothing fancy, just an indoor/outdoor type with rubber backing, but in as playful a pattern and as bright a color as I could find.

"I know why the kids are always under foot," I reasoned to John. "They need a nice big area to play in. We can move the toy box your Dad built; the doll furniture that you made; the Tonka trucks (Don't ask whatever possessed me to keep this collection in a bedroom) and, during the winter months, even their riding toys, if we make an attractive play room in the basement."

John fell for it, just as I had. And so we set to work creating a section of the basement sure to capture our little ones' attention. My plan was to fill it with every inviting toy, leaving few but the cuddly and soft for upstairs and bedrooms.

Soon our basement was divided just as I had devised with the wash tubs and laundry in one area; my sewing machine, cabinets, and needed tables for pattern lay outs in another section; a walled off work room confining tools, stored paint cans and "stuff" in a third area; and finally, and most importantly, what became "The K's version of Playland," which covered the remainder of the basement.

Our cozy looking and colorful remnant rug now neatly contained an assortment (thanks to John's craftsmanship and my garage sale bargains), of attractively arranged furniture for "little people," as well as dolls, dishes, dress-up clothes; Tinker Toys, Lincoln Logs, Legos and Duplos (regular and large size); along with Tim, Charlie and Tony's "machinery hill" an array of miniature tractors, army tanks, trucks, Hot Wheel cars, and what seemed like hundreds of little characters to match. You get the picture.

I figured they'd descend down that flight of stairs never to be seen again until age 18, or at least dinnertime!

"I'll bet this play site will be the biggest draw in the neighborhood," I naively boasted.

Guess again. It was not—even on the most rainy, stormy, blistering hot, tornado threatening, freezing cold, or snowed-in wintery of days! Unless, of course, I was in the same area!

"I can't believe it. We create this terrific playroom, and here they sit at the other end of the basement on the cold, damp floor next to me, pulling open my cabinets, while I'm trying to sew," I reluctantly reported to Johnny by week's end.

"Isn't that nice, they want to be near you," John calmly responded.

Cute isn't he?

"You'd think they'd be thrilled with their own little section. But no! Instead, they got into my cabinets, unravelled my spools of thread, and then Tina took the pinking sheers to Tony's bangs while I was busy with the laundry," I whined.

All in all, "Playland Basement" taught me a powerful lesson in mothering: no matter how educational or enticing the toy, how inviting the room, or how many children there were to fill it, small youngsters would sooner pick up their playthings and settle at mom's feet, than be holed up and separated from her.

Later on of course, the scene changes, and they go to all sorts of lengths to create isolation, preferring privacy; alone-time behind closed bedroom doors; and outings with peers not parents. That's when the tables are turned and we work to stay close to them.

In other words, cherish the now. "Cling free" comes only too soon.

Yes, Johnny was right. Children play and behave better; are calmer and certainly feel more secure, when Mom is nearby.

Ask any mother with a toddler who has tried to get through a dinner hour without her little one close by. And isn't it something how they prefer kitchen utensils and Mom's pots and pans to almost any fancy toy?

As they grow older, the same principle applies. How many moms have kids who bound through the door after school each day, calling her name? Not that they necessarily want to talk to her, tell about their day, or offer anything more than one syllable responses to questions. It's simply the assurance of knowing "Mom's here for me!"

Good parents do all in their power to love and reassure their young. Sometimes it may come in the form of discipline (also love). It can also appear at all hours!

When youngsters are small, we slip into their bedrooms at night to check on them. We see that windows are closed if it's cold, kiss them, and tuck them in. We make sure they are all right.

When they grow older, we set boundaries and curfews (to keep our sanity). We worry frantically if they are late, waiting up until they return. All the while praying as we pace a cold kitchen floor.

That's what good parenting is all about.

In a way, big people are much like little ones. We search for and cling to comfort, security, and a sense that "I will be taken care of."

Unfortunately, sometimes we look in all the wrong places: power, prestige, property, or perhaps people. Each of us has a longing almost like a hole in our heart, for something or someone greater who will "watch over me."

The answer, of course, is Faith. And it doesn't resemble anything close to "Playland Basement" separation. Our Heavenly Father wants us to be close, happy and *with Him* for all eternity.

Christ promised, *"Know that I am with you always until the end of the world" (Matthew* 28:20). And He shows us each day in a thousand different ways that He loves us and wants to fill in that "hole" or emptiness, with His love.

Psalm 121 says it best: *"The Lord is your guardian; The Lord will guard you from all evil; He will guard your life. The Lord will guard your coming and your going, both now and forever" (Psalm* 121: 5-8).

And to think, all we need do is stay close to Him and ask.

"For You are my hope, O Lord; my trust, O God, from my youth. On You I depend from birth; from my mother's womb You are my strength" (Psalm 71:5-6).

Barbecued Pork Chops
(When I'm feeling lazy)

Lean Pork Chops
Onion—chopped
1 tsp Ketchup—over each chop
1 Tbsp Brown sugar—over each chop
Tobasco sauce—shake over each chop

Place chops in baking dish covering each one with ketchup, brown sugar, chopped onion and a squirt of Tobasco sauce. Cover tightly with tin foil and bake slowly (325-350°) for 45 min. Uncover and baste often (add water to juice if necessary) till chops are browned and thoroughly cooked.

Serve with white or wild rice. It looks and tastes as if you've been fussing all day. (Okay, so it's cheating!)

CHAPTER 2

Do You Belong To "Atoms"?

"Children, obey your parents in the Lord, for that is what is expected of you. 'Honor your father and mother' is the first commandment to carry a promise with it—that it may go well with you, and that you may have long life on the earth" (*Ephesians* 6:1-3).

Have you ever wondered who all the other moms are? I have. I hear about them from my kids every time I say no to something they want to do. It usually begins with, "But all the other moms let their kids. . ." (fill in the blank).

I think they have a regular organization but I've never been invited to join. In my house they're simply known as "**A**ll **T**he **O**ther **M**oms." I call them **ATOMs.**

Take the other day, for example. I was "awesome" and got a warm hug because I said, "Yes" to a sleep-over for my 13 year-old and her two friends. *A note to the naive: a sleep-over is an adolescent event where anything remotely resembling "sleep" is *never* experienced!

Then later, when I said, "No" to a PG-13 movie, my halo broke, I fell from grace, and I was instantly told about "**A**ll **T**he **O**ther **M**oms."

Now don't get me wrong, my kids are good and, by and large, they are quite obedient, never sassing or arguing too strenuously or disrespectfully once they see it's hopeless.

Yet there's no ignoring the sulking body, the sighs of suppression, the glazed eyes, the folded arms, or that far-away look. Every one of my kids from tot to teen has demonstrated the symptoms at one time or another. And it always means the same whether they think it or dare to say it: "Why can't you be like All The Other Moms?"

"Why can't they be like me?" Now there's a scarey thought!

In one of my more frenzied and impassioned moments, when one of my kids hit me with, "But all the other moms let their kids," I naively asked for their names and numbers, only to learn that All The Other Moms have no last name, no permanent address and no recognizable identity. They're just "All The Other Moms."

ATOM's, so I've been told, is comprised of progressive open-minded parents. These modern-day guardians seem to be up on the latest, and committed to values no more far reaching than "responsible use." No such thing as "tough love" for these parents!

Unlike me, they are trendy folks who understand and *trust* their offspring. No need to supervise, discipline, or set limits for their kids. ATOMs live in the '90s! No rules for their children. Responsibility and reason reign supreme. Never mind that kids need guidance and absolutes, and that's why God gave them parents.

God? Who said anything about God?

You can well imagine how "out-of-it" I feel with all my conditions and consequences, compared to All the Other Moms who offer "feel good" values and *unconditional* love. (As if there was any other kind).

There's no denying, however, that taking our parenting role seriously as God intended, has its pitfalls.

Take for instance, the time I met Mrs. Loomis at a Church social and she opened the conversation with, "Mrs. Kuharski—congratulations!"

When I asked "What for?" she responded, "I understand you were just elected President."

"President of what?" I sarcastically inquired knowing I vowed no new committees that Spring.

"President of the Mean Mothers' Club. Your two boys, Tim and Charlie nominated you just yesterday. But, don't feel too badly, I was elected Vice President by my son."

So much for precious moments.

Any of you Moms or Dads who have struggled like my husband and me, standing firm in areas of faith, morals, common sense, hygiene, and general decency when challenged by their children and All The Other Moms, you know the meaning of the word *heartburn.*

If you are still clinging by your weary fingernails to old-fashioned modes of parenting and discipline—insisting on virtue, manners, curfews, decency, respect and—here's a big-gie—obedience—you're not alone.

In my case, it's taken years of experience to realize the only remedy is time, patience, prayer (yes, I do, and often) and maturity—not mine, but theirs. As the prophets of old wisely advise, "This too will pass."

And so it does! The sulking, pouting, disappointed child gets over it; Tim and Charlie grow to adulthood; and with the passage of time, most of us rejects from **ATOMs**, suddenly and magically appear to have more insight and wisdom than either child or parent ever suspected.

The same sons who once elected me president of the Mean Mothers' Club and vowed that I was unlike All The Other Moms because of my archaic attitude, have now moved into that wonderful new phase called *maturity.*

And what do they think of me now? In their view, Mom has suddenly turned "pushover" where their younger brothers and sisters are concerned. No more All The Other Moms. It's Tim and Charlie who are frequently heard saying, "Boy, when I was your age we never got by with that!" "Mom's turned into a real *marshmallow!*" Or "Ya mean Dad and Mom let you _____?" (fill in the blank). "We never could!"

Has all this sticking to principles been worth it? All I can say is, "All The Other Moms eat your hearts out!"

A few guiding principles we've learned along the way:

• **Stick to your standards and principles.** Never waver in areas of faith and morals. Your children will always know where you stand, even if they don't always appreciate your decision at the time, you will at least have their respect. A "wishy-washy" adult is held in little esteem by young people.

• **Respect your children's ideas and opinions.** Listen to what your children have to say, but be true to what you know is right and in your children's best interest. Be sensitive to their feelings, and your judgment will be more accepted.

• **Compromise** *can* **be helpful in some situations, as long as it never involves issues of morality.** I don't mind bending on the little inconsequential things that don't really matter. However, in situations where I believe my child's health, both physical and spiritual, may be adversely affected, I am known as "cement."

• **Contact the other moms or dads.** There is strength in numbers. In some situations, it is best to connect with other parents to come up with a plan that will be best for *all the youngsters* involved. And most parents are genuinely grateful for the supportive network.

• **Give it time**. Time, even just 24 hours helps everyone put things in perspective. Kids get over things faster than adults. They are also quick to move on and to forgive hurts.

• **Pray.** God promises parents the grace necessary for every situation. Ask Jesus to take over and take charge. Pray to your child's patron saint and guardian angel. You could be accused of "ganging up." You bet! But make no mistake: prayer works.

"Therefore, take these words of mine into your heart and soul. Bind them at your wrist as a sign, and let them be a pendant on your forehead. Teach them to your children, speaking of them at home and abroad, whether you are busy or at rest" (*Deuteronomy* 11:18-19).

Aunt Dolores' Pizza Hot Dish
Great for large groups or parties

8 oz pkg Egg Noodles	Fennel seed—to taste
2 lbs Ground beef	2 tsp Salt
2 large Onions	1/4 tsp Pepper
2 Cups Chopped Celery	1 tsp Oregano
1 15 oz can Tomato Sauce	2 tsp Brown sugar
2 large Cans of Tomatoes	Cheddar Cheese—grated
	Mozerella Cheese—grated

Brown meat. Add celery, onions and cook till tender. Mix tomatoes and spices together. It is not necessary to cook noodles before placing in hotdish—but I do until they are slightly limp. Put in layers in loaf pan:

Rotating sauce, meat, noodles, and cheese. Repeat layers, ending with cheese topping. Bake for 2 hours at 325°. (Or higher temp for lesser time.) I cover for the first half of baking time. (You may spoon bottom over top mixture so as not to dry out.)

* I love Fennel Seed so it usually finds its way in just about every Italian thing I concoct!

CHAPTER 3

Adoption Is Biblical And Part Of God's Plan

"I drew them with human cords, with bands of love; I fostered them like one who raises an infant to his cheeks" (*Hosea* 11:4).

Growing up as an adopted kid, I was often told by my parents that I was "twice loved," once by the mother who carried me and gave me life, and again by my adopted Mom and Dad. I believed them.

Being raised in a good northeast Minneapolis household with strong Catholic and ethnic/Italian roots, neither I nor my two adopted brothers nor any other kid I hung around with ever knew there was such a thing as an "unwanted child." Nuisance yes, but "unwanted" never!

Adoption to me was God's way of bringing children and parents together!

Today I am the mother of many, nearly half of whom came to us, not by my "tummy," but by adoption. And what a blessing it has been to all of us. We are a *family* in every sense. Even in a household of varied skin colors and cultures, it's hard to remember we are not "blood related."

Yet, even with a multiracial flair, adoption can become status-quo and hohum. I can still remember the chuckles at the Sunday breakfast table when our newly adopted son Charlie, blurted out, "Gosh, did you guys ever notice that all the Makowskes look alike?" Charlie thought *all families* were mixed race.

Another time, five-year-old Kari, a "tummy" kid, asked, "Tell me about my adoption" and we broke the news, "Honey, you came from Mom and Dad."

The day we moved to our newer and larger home located down the street from our church and school, our daughter Tina, ran home to announce, "Hey good news! We're not the only ones on the block with a big family. The people down the street have eight kids. But guess what—not one of them is adopted!"

Poor dears!

My mother always told me that my adoption was "part of God's plan" and as I grew in maturity and faith, I came to know that it was the courage and grace of my birthmother's action in making an adoption decision, that really fulfilled His plan. The rest is up to me.

I also believe that the children placed in our hearts and homes, whether by adoption or birth, are only ours *temporarily*. It then becomes our primary goal to help them know their Heavenly Father and to aim them toward Heaven. Easier said than done, I might add.

In my biased view, adoption should be promoted, portrayed, and praised for the life saving and loving act that it is. Most pro-life counselors who see women in crisis pregnancy situations are saddened by the anti-adoption mindset that controls decision making. Many women say, "I have two choices. Keep *it* or abortion. I could never give up my own flesh and blood."

When did America change it's attitude toward adoption? With over 1.6 million women having abortions each year and over half of them repeats we know that each time adoption is rejected and abortion *chosen*, a baby is killed.

Worse yet, according to the National Council for Adoption, "two million couples are waiting to adopt"—that's forty couples for every available baby, including infants of all races and those with special needs.

One of the most disheartening effects of the abortionizing of America, is the anti-adoption attitude which has spilled

over to otherwise good people who, by their language and
behavior help to discourage, distort, or denigrate the option of
adoption.

According to a survey by the National Women's Coalition
for Life, as reported by the National Council for Adoption
(NCFA), one of the primary reasons that clients choose abortion over adoption, according to pregnancy counselors, is
because "adoption appears too difficult (practically or emotionally)."

"In the media climate of the past fifteen years, where a
vocal group of birthmothers have positioned themselves on
television talk shows discussing the regrets they have about
their adoption decisions, it is not surprising," reports NCFA,
"that adoption appears too difficult."

Added to that are the counselors who admit their own dis-
comfort in discussing adoption, due perhaps to anti-adoption
propaganda or misinformation. Remember too, abortion is rel-
atively quick, final and *over* by comparison.

NCFA states that "women who could benefit from adoption
are being denied the opportunity to discuss it fully. Or, in many
cases, simply to be offered full and adequate information about
adoption."

Adding to the frailty of adoption are the lawyers and judges
who overturn legally binding contracts, convincing the
American public that adoption is risky, debatable and may not
be *forever*. The results are heartrending stories of little ones
taken from their legally adoptive families (some after many
years) because of a birthparent's change of mind.

Negative views of adoption are often received through TV
talk shows, soap operas, or at the kitchen table by well-meaning family or friends. Few young people will be led to believe
that adoption is a beautiful and loving act if they only hear
stories of birth mothers living in lifelong regret or are led to
believe that adopted children are maladjusted and searching, as
has been sadly sensationalized by organized anti-adoption
groups and portrayed through the dominant secular media.

When these same young people have friends or themselves are confronted by an untimely pregnancy it is little wonder that abortion becomes the quickest and easiest option of choice, with keeping the baby as a harrowing second; while the option of adoption is all but dismissed.

Christians know that adoption is Biblical. Scripture reminds us continually: *"God sent forth His Son, born of a woman, born under the law, to deliver from the law, those who were subjected to it, so that we might receive our status as adopted sons"* (*Galatians* 4:4-5).

In fact, we are *children of destiny.* **God has a mission and a purpose for each of us.** Therefore, we must never allow negative talk regarding adoption. Such talk denigrates God's plan. Worse, it can actually result in a pregnant and frightened woman choosing abortion.

Moses is perhaps one of the most outstanding Biblical examples of adoption. It was his birthmother who, acting for fear of his life, and trusting God's intervention, placed him in a basket in the river. And it was Pharaoh's sister, after discovering the abandoned child afloat on the water, who brought him to her brother where he was raised as Pharaoh's own son.

It was in this adoptive environment that Moses learned the leadership skills necessary to bring the Israelites from slavery in Egypt into freedom.

What can we do to counteract the anti-adoption mindset? As Christians, by our word and witness we can promote the goodness of adoption:

• A note of encouragement or an "I'm praying for you" hug offers support and strength to those contemplating an adoption decision.

• Always talk positively about adoption as the loving and unselfish act that it is. Your children, family, and friends are listening.

• Write your elected Congressmen and urge support of adoption policies which offer pregnant women a *real* choice, as well as a tax break for couples who adopt, making it affordable for middle or lower income families.

• Pray daily for the pregnant and undecided mother, and for her vulnerable child who wants only the opportunity to be born.

Psalm 139 reminds us, *"Truly you have formed my inmost being; you knit me in my mother's womb. I give you thanks that I am fearfully, wonderfully made; wonderful are your works. My soul also you knew full well."*

Those of us who know personally the blessings of adoption cherish those words. We also hope you will join us in portraying the goodness of adoption and it's message of life and love.

"Whoever welcomes one such child for my sake welcomes me. On the other hand, it would be better for anyone who leads astray one of these little ones who believe in me, to be drowned by a millstone around his neck, in the depths of the sea" (*Matthew* 18:5-6).

Aunt Catherine's Goulash
Charlie's Favorite

1 lb Ground Beef	Salt & Pepper to taste
1 can of Tomato Soup	Ketchup to taste
1 onion—or more	Chopped Celery—as you like
1 pkg Elbow Macaroni	1/2 can Water—to thin

Fry meat and onion until browned. Then add chopped celery, salt, and pepper, ketchup, Tomato soup, and water. Cook noodles till tender and mix in with meat sauce thoroughly till mixed and serve.

* This is so basic and simple—but still one of our kids favorite! I like it because you can throw it together at the last minute. Charlie downs two full plates when he comes home.

CHAPTER 4

A Blessing For Expectant Mothers

"Behold, children are a gift from the Lord; the fruit of the womb is a reward. Like arrows in the hand of a warrior are the children of one's youth. Happy the man whose quiver is filled with them" (*Psalm* 127:3-5).

One of the most memorable things that happened to me as a young mother-to-be, was receiving the "Blessing for Expectant Mothers." Though I've experienced many years and many children since that Blessing, it is an event I look back to and remember as profoundly significant. (There are those who might suggest the Blessing itself is responsible for the fruitfulness we so abundantly received.)

The blessing came with our first baby. I certainly had my share of apprehension about what pregnancy and motherhood represented. Not just because we were young, or because our finances were less than secure as we budgeted in our rented upper duplex and depended upon my legal secretary salary while my husband John, worked full-time toward his college degree. But after all, motherhood would mean a whole new way of life for me. Little did I dream!

I probably never realized at the time, the full impact of having a priest praying over me. Yet, even at that naive moment the very gesture itself brought home the mystery in which I was chosen to participate.

Yes, there is a grace that is released from such a sacramental that offers protection, guidance, and strength.

The ceremony is simple, and the prayers are short. One petition says, "May Christ fill your heart with His holy joy and keep you and your baby safe from harm."

Another is from *Isaiah 44:3: "I will pour out water upon the thirsty ground, and streams upon the dry land; I will pour out my spirit upon your offspring, and my blessing upon your descendants."*

To me, the blessing served as a reminder. It told me that more than John and I were involved here. Along with a sense of peace came a keen awareness of God and His part in this miracle of new human life.

The very ritual of the blessing stirs in all observers: family, friends, Catholic, and non-Catholic alike, a sacredness and solemnity. There's a miracle going on here.

The focus of the blessing is not just on the pregnancy or health, but on the hereafter: *"Receive with kindness the prayer of your servant as she asks for the birth of a healthy child. Grant that she may safely deliver a son or a daughter to be numbered among Your family, to serve You in all things and to gain eternal life."* (Book of Blessings)

Is there a mother who wouldn't welcome such a prayer?

Whatever happened to the Blessing for Expectant Mothers?

We don't hear much about it nowadays. This is particularly unfortunate because we are surrounded by a society which weighs a child's "worthiness" solely upon its "wantedness," rather than on seeing each as made in the very image and likeness of God.

It seems to me that such a blessing is needed now more than ever.

Perhaps the most positive thing we can do as pro-life Catholics is to give witness to our love of life and family. What better way to do this than welcoming a new baby into our lives and celebrating that expectant "little one" (*fetus* in Latin) with the bestowing of a blessing on all expectant mothers.

By effort and example we can counteract the anti-life concept that tolerates *only* the perfect, planned, and the wanted.

Each time we welcome new life and encourage our children and family to do the same, we reject the cynicism and negativism regarding large families that permeates society.

Each time we teach our young to pray for pregnant mothers tempted by abortion and to spiritually adopt their baby, we combat the abortion tide and overpopulation lies that go against God's truth.

Sad to say, many expectant mothers have been intimidated and ridiculed by strangers, and even supposedly pro-life friends who challenge, "Pregnant again! Isn't that enough?"

New parents need our support and encouragement. If each of us would give an expectant couple, including those in the process of adoption, a hug of support, and a suggestion to our parish community to re-introduce and encourage the once often-used Blessing for Expectant Mothers, our witness would be far reaching indeed.

We may not change the laws, but we can change hearts. And that change occurs most often between individuals, one heartbeat to another, rather than through massive movements.

Is this blessing familiar to you? Why not mention it to your pastor? Most are only too pleased to reintroduce it to parishioners. And why not tell other young couples—especially those expecting or planning to adopt?

It's a simple sacramental that can be performed just about anywhere, in a home by a visiting priest (a great way to invite a priest for dinner) or before or after Sunday Mass.

Catholics used to have a corner on blessings. We still do. We have them for holidays, feast days, harvest time, and just about *any* time. In this age mesmerized by hate and death, what better way to demonstrate love and life than to pray as a church community for those preparing to welcome one of God's most precious little ones.

"A gracious wife delights her husband, her thoughtfulness puts flesh on his bones; a gift from the Lord is her governed

speech, and her firm virtue is of surpassing worth.

    Choicest of blessings is a modest wife, priceless her chaste person.

    Like the sun rising in the Lord's heavens, the beauty of a virtuous wife is the radiance of her home.

    Like the light which shines above the holy lampstand, are her beauty of face and graceful figure" (*Sirach* 26:13-17).

Chicken Pot Pie
(My Version)

1 Cup cubed, cooked Chicken

1 (16 oz) bag frozen vegetable combination (Cauliflower, Carrots, Broccoli, thawed

1-2 Peeled Potatoes (par-cooked and diced)

1-2 Carrots, par-cooked & diced

3-4 Green Onion, chopped fine

1-2 Celergy stalks

1 2.8 oz can Durkee French Fried Onions

1 Can Cream of Chicken Soup

1/2 Cup Milk

1/2 tsp Seasoned Salt

Salt and Pepper

Marjoram

1 Cup shredded Cheddar Cheese

1 9-inch Pie Crust (unbaked)

1 sm Green Pepper (if desired)

    Par cook or microwave fresh veggies (potatoes, onions, carrots, celery). Preheat oven to 400°. Combine diced chicken, vegetables, soup, milk, spices, cheese, and French fried onions in bowl. Stir together and pour over unbaked pie crust in 9-inch pie plate. Seal edges and cut 4 steam vents. Place on sheet to catch any overflow (it always happens at this house) and bake at 400 for 40 minutes. If crust gets too dark, cover w. tin foil.

CHAPTER 5

Baptism And Godparents— A Spiritual Force

"Go therefore and make disciples of all nations. Baptize them in the name of the Father and of the Son and of the Holy Spirit. Teach them to carry out everything I have commanded you. And know that I am with you always, until the end of the world!" (Matthew 28:19-20).

Being a godparent—or choosing one—is a pretty big deal.

Speaking from personal experience, it doesn't have to be a person who promises to spend a lot of time with a child. Although, that's always nice.

And it doesn't have to be someone who is prepared to "take the child if something happens to the parents"—a notion held by many in years past.

No. A godparent is a person who promises to demonstrate a "spiritual concern" for the one being baptized. Sounds easy at first. But according to the *Catechism of the Catholic Church* "For the grace of Baptism to unfold, the parents' help is important. So too, is the role of the godfather and godmother, who must be firm believers, able and ready to help the newly baptized—child or adult—on the road of Christian life."

And the reason most Baptisms take place today during the Sunday liturgy is because it involves all of us. In fact, the *Catechism* reminds us that "The whole ecclesiastical community bears some responsibility for the development and safe-guarding of the grace given at Baptism."

What a wonderful thought for parents to know that *every-one* in the community is praying for the spiritual well-being of their newly baptized baby—in addition to the chosen godpar-ents. When John and I became parents we wanted the Baptism to be remembered as joyous and a very special occasion. Our family looked forward to them with great fanfare. (Some accuse me of having all these children just so we could have another party.)

Yep, I do like to party, and we did celebrate. Yet, we never lost sight of the *real* meaning of the event. In fact, our parties merely accented the specialness and importance of the occa-sion.

It is also a great time to explain to the other children about the promises we made *for them* at their own Baptism and the meaning of the Sacrament. Sometimes our kids needed a little refresher.

"We have to get the baby baptized so she can live in America," our young adopted Vietnamese son, Tony, once explained to a kid sister.

Another, trying to correct his error, piped in, "No. It's so's ya can vote!"

Obviously we had some explaining to do.

The *Catechism* teaches that "The faith required for Baptism is not a perfect and *mature faith*, but a beginning that is called to develop."

"To develop" that's where parents and those wonderful god-parents come in.

Godparents can't always be present in a youngster's life, but we can discipline ourselves to act as spiritual guardians by remembering to pray **often** for our godchildren. We can ask their own Guardian Angels to stay close by and to protect them from harm.

My own Godmother had a large family of her own and very little time or money to spare. Yet, she was there for my First Communion, Confirmation, graduations, and Wedding.

I received no fancy gifts over the years, but she did call me periodically and was genuinely interested in what I was doing. Kids remember that. More than that, she would end our conversation after asking the usual, "How are you?"; "What's new?"; and "Any new boyfriends?"; with "Now remember, Be good. I'm your Godmother and you're pretty special!"

Her call was always uplifting and always a boost.

Many touchy or tough questions may surround the birth of a new baby, dealing with everything from diapers, and discipline, to parenting essentials and, later, the child's education. But none is more important than a child's spiritual welfare. After all, as parents our number one goal is not to provide for everything *here* but to guide them toward the *hereafter.*

Sometimes we tend to think of choosing a godparent as a special favor or prize demonstrating our closeness or affection. While there is certainly nothing wrong with that, it is important to ask ourselves as new parents, which of our family and friends would best help us pray for our child's spiritual well being? And are they good role models for our child to look up to?

Kids today are inundated with temptations and adults who sell them short or offer them mixed and double messages, especially in the area of morality and faith.

We want to remind them that we believe in them, that God loves them, and that He will give them the grace necessary for *every* situation. Godparents can help us do that.

Speaking of Baptism, what about that family member or loved one who brings a baby into the world and has no intention of Baptizing the infant. It's happened in our family and, quite honestly, I am always tempted to grab the kid, run into the bathroom and dunk 'em under the faucet before anyone can stop me! "Wouldn't that still count?" I painfully wrestle with myself.

Yet, I know I can't take away the parents primary *right* to guide their child. Even if I'm a sister, grandmother, or close relative or friend.

It doesn't mean I can't talk to them, tell them of my concern for the child, and to *pray*—pray hard. And that's just what I'm doing.

Because Baptism is the incorporation into Christ and the Christian community, it implies certain obligations such as leading a Christian life and being faithful to the laws of God and the Church. Leading a Christian life and a desire for eternal life with Christ hereafter, may never be realized, however, if the parent stubbornly abandons the faith.

Perhaps, in these instances, we can be "spiritual godparents of desire" (I made this up) praying and pleading that the responsible parent, come back to the fold and Baptize the child.

As a mom of many, I am grateful for the godparents who have been good role models and guides in my own children's lives. Their willingness to be such a positive presence has made me realize all the more what a spiritual force godparents are meant to be!

"Then He told them: "Go into the whole world and proclaim the good news to all creation. The man who believes in it and accepts baptism will be saved; the man who refuses to believe in it will be condemned" (Mark 16:15-16).

Chicken & Broccoli Hot Dish
Chrissy's Favorite

Broccoli Spears (par-cooked)
A few carrots (for color) (slightly par cooked)
Onion—chopped large (slightly par cooked)
Cooked Chicken (in large chunks)
1 C Cream of Mushroom Soups
1 C Cream of Chicken Soup
1 Cup Miracle Whip
Cheddar Cheese (shredded)
1/2 Can Water to thin
1/4 tsp Thyme
Marjoram, dash
Croutons for topping
1/4 tsp Curry Powder (I never seem to have this on hand.)

Put broccoli, carrots, and onion on bottom of pan. Place chicken on top. Mix soups, spices, and water together in bowl. Spread grated cheese over chicken and broccoli, pour mixture on top. Top with croutons and more cheese (if desired) Bake at 350° for 35—45 min.
Let set—then serve.

CHAPTER 6

John Paul II Encourages New Mothers To Breast-Feed

"My being proclaims the greatness of the Lord. my spirit finds joy in God my savior" (*Luke* 1:46-47).

Pope John Paul II has an opinion on breast-feeding? Yep. And as always, he is sensitive, futuristic, and right on target!

Specifically, the Holy Father said breast-feeding "is of interest to the church because it deals with the vital interaction between mother and child," (*"Pope urges worldwide support for breastfeeding" Catholic Bulletin* May 18, 1995) and because it raises larger health and economic issues especially in developing nations.

Bravo! It comes at a much-needed time as increasing data confirm that breast-feeding is losing favor. In the "progressive" United States, researchers note that Hispanic or migrant women intent on imitating what they perceive as the "American way" are choosing to bottle-feed in greater numbers.

On a global scale, surveys show that around the world, two-thirds of women still breast-feed, but the number is decreasing.

There is no debating the fact that breast milk offers a host of vitamins and nutrition to an infant far superior to any bottled commercial formula. No doubt Pope John Paul II took this into consideration, as well as the hazards of contaminated water and issues of poor hygiene which make bottle-feeding risky in underdeveloped countries.

Choosing to breast-feed is more than just a sound nutritional choice. It offers the infant something all humans crave, holding, snuggling, and loving. And by whom better than mom?

Yet, even within the medical community support is lacking. Judith W. Vogelhut, R.N., a consultant at the Johns Hopkins Children's Center Breast-Feeding Clinic, stated in a report in *Family Practice News* (5-95), "Some physicians hesitate to advocate breast-feeding, feeling that they should remain neutral."

Vogelhut chided colleagues, "You would not feel the need to be neutral if the mother was a smoker."

What a shame, considering that every major study has proven that babies who are breast-fed, according to a 1995 *Medical Tribune* report, "have a lower rate of infection and contagious disease" and thrive better than bottle-fed infants.

In fact, the report states "the protective effects of breast-feeding persisted for one year even when breast-feeding stopped at thirteen weeks."

The real shocker, according to a John Hopkins study which compared IQ data on breast-fed and bottle-fed infants is that "Even intelligence is aided by breast-feeding."

"Hmmm, we'll see," says this Mom.

Perhaps the point here has more to do with a child's sense of security, wantedness, and self-worth.

Especially beneficial to premature infants, studies show that "preterm babies fed breast milk have a reduced hospital stay, quicker weight gain, and better stabilization of respiration and cardiac cycles," according to Dr. Linda Black of the Pediatric Clinic of North Little Rock, Arkansas.

So why the reluctance to breast-feed?

The answer may rest not with the mother but with the father, according to another study from Johns Hopkins: "The father's favorable opinion about breast-feeding is the single strongest determinant of whether a woman chooses to nurse her newborn."

One pediatric specialist, Dr. Jay A. Perman, suggested, "So maybe we can encourage breast-feeding by targeting the fathers more than we do."

When it comes down to it, many a young mother will chose to bottle-feed simply because she was never encouraged to consider the benefits of breast-feeding. Close family and friends can make a positive difference.

Researchers and mothers alike recognize the important psychological bond that is established between mother and child which, though intangible, forms a foundation for love that will unite them the rest of their lives. Certainly, this is what Pope John Paul II had in mind.

Personally speaking, the act also involves what millions of nursing moms know to be one of the most fulfilling and rewarding experiences. In my view—after nine months of pregnancy, labor, delivery, and what seemed like a "drive-by" hospital stay—breast-feeding was God's little bonus! Just to take the time each day, no matter the chores that surrounded me, to sit and snuggle my new baby brought an indescribable reward never imagined.

I also found it a natural and excellent teaching tool. I remember when my two eight-year-old boys discovered what breast-feeding meant: "Ya mean moms can even do that too!" our Tim once remarked in wide-eyed surprise.

Hearing of the Pope's recent declaration reminded me of my own nervousness and apprehension as a new mother attempting to nurse our first newborn. Not helping matters, she was colicky.

Most intimidating were the remarks made by well-meaning family or friends who'd say, "Boy, you *are* 'old fashioned' aren't you?" or "Gosh, doesn't that tie you down a lot?"

Lucky for me I had three strong allies, my husband, my mother, and my mother-in-law. Yet, my father was embarrassed, even though I was entirely covered. At the sight, he would turn and walk out of the room, saying to my mother, "Does she have to do that? Can't she use a bottle?"

Dad was accustomed to the "modern way" and breast-feeding contrary to being the natural thing to do, seemed *unnatural* and primitive.

Nancy, a young mother of four recalls, "I never thought of breast-feeding with my first. Why didn't anyone tell me?" After she was introduced to the concept, she quickly became a staunch advocate.

"It's not only easier, no bottles, formula mixing, packing a day's supply for an outing, or walking on a cold kitchen floor to fetch a bottle at 3:00 AM," she says, "it's also inexpensive and you have all the equipment you need right on you. But, the *real* benefit," she adds, "is the wonderful closeness I feel toward this baby. I really regret not nursing the others."

Not every mother *can* breast-feed. I couldn't nurse our six adopted kids. For others, there may be health or working schedules that prevent their ability to breast-feed.

But, let's not hesitate to do what Pope John Paul II has done, offer encouragement and support, for those mothers who can breast-feed.

Perhaps if the world saw more mommies snuggling their young in public we would be more mindful of the tenderness, affection, and love so vital to family life. This is an all but misplaced or forgotten reality in today's fast-paced frantic world. Far more prominent are the constant statistics which reveal an ever-increasing number of children who are victims of abuse, abandonment, and abortion.

Pope John Paul II is strong and constant in his support of human life and what we know to be the "Domestic Church"— the family. His declaration on breast-feeding is but one more beautiful example. This mom says, "Hooray!"

"Jesus turned to them and said: 'Daughters of Jerusalem, do not weep for me. Weep for yourselves and for your children. The days are coming when they will say, "Happy are the sterile, the wombs that never bore and the breasts that never nursed"'" (*Luke* 23:28-30).

Cindy's "Never Fail" Popovers

1 Cup Milk
3 Tbsp Vegetable Oil
3 Eggs
1 tsp Salt
1 Cup Flour

Beat eggs, milk, and oil together with a wisk real good. Add salt and flour. Pour in well greased popover tins (they do not rise well in muffin pans) Bake in hot 400° oven for 30 minutes. (Popovers, at our house, are relished like dessert!)

CHAPTER 7

Let's Hear It For The At-Home Mom

"When one finds a worthy wife, her value is far beyond pearls. Her husband, entrusting his heart to her, has an unfailing prize. She brings him good, and not evil, all the days of her life. She reaches out her hands to the poor, and extends her arms to the needy. She fears not the snow for her household; all her charges are doubly clothed. She is clothed with strength and dignity, and she laughs at the days to come. She opens her mouth in wisdom, and on her tongue is kindly counsel. She watches the conduct of her household, and eats not her food in idleness. Her children rise up and praise her; her husband too, extols her: 'Many are the women of proven worth, but you have excelled them all.' Charm is deceptive and beauty fleeting; the woman who fears the Lord is to be praised" (Proverbs *31:10-12, 20-21, 25-30).*

Most of us stay-at-home moms have stiff-lipped it through more than our share of the "I'll bet it was hard to give up your career" queries. They don't know our kids are worth every sacrifice made to live on one paycheck.

"You're on a leave of absence, of course." Assuming *no* contemporary woman stays home after a respectable period of leave. "Not **full-time?**" some reply when I tell them my *occupation.* "You must do *something* else with your time," one lady recently told me. When I asked her *why,* it was her turn to be speechless.

29

I get a kick out of the "Long Range Interrogator": "You **do** plan to go back to work as soon as they're all in school?" Presumably the job must be over by then, and anything less than re-entry into the working world is unquestionably slumming!

In truth, my kids need the presence of mom the minute they hit the back door after school. I want them to know I'm here if they pass the test, won the ribbon, caught the mumps, flunked the class, need a ride, got sent to the principal's office (yep, it's happened), or just need Mom.

One of my least favorite questions is what I call the "Goose's Golden Egg": "*Your* husband must be making a *very* good living." I like them to think we're independently wealthy and only shop with coupons and drive old vans just for fun.

Most inquirers are well-meaning and simply echo, without thinking, a culture and system that's led us to believe all moms need or have *other* careers. This is in no way meant to be disrespectful of the mothers who work part-time or those who truly *must* work.

Yet, long overdue is society's acknowledgment, support, and respect of the stay-at-home mom and the sacrifices made by *both* her and her husband.

Each time a Christian husband is willing to make that sacrifice and carry the financial load, with a wife who forgoes outside second career and income, they give a loving witness to the vocational call of motherhood.

I remember my shock and disappointment the day one of my own college-age daughters called home and matter-of-factly asked, "Mom, didn't you resent giving up your career to stay home and take care of us kids?"

My real disappointment was that she even had to ask.

Just wait til that same skeptical daughter falls in love and the product of that love, her baby, is handed to her on the delivery table, or through the process of adoption. Will there be a promotion or paycheck that could match such an experience? "*Not!*" as my kids would say.

Most reasonable people agree that **what children need most**

is a sense of security, continuity, and the ever-present love that is best expressed by a full-time mother in the home. Yes, as politically incorrect as it seems, I did say "mother."

My own daughter's question about the importance of full-time mothering raised its own question: What are our schools teaching children about the value of motherhood? And what happens if they succeed?

As a young, somewhat inexperienced mom, I once thought my nurturing role would be less needed "full-time" when my kids were all in school. My friend, Pat, an older and wiser mom of experience set me straight: "When they enter the adolescent and teen years, Mary Ann, they need you all the more. But in a different way. Many a time I was grateful to have been there when my kids came in the door from school and I was able to be there and offer a listening ear or to head off trouble before it took over." Pat was right!

In two decades time America has experienced a total turn around in attitude and respect with regard to what was once universally understood to be, as more than one United States President has described, the "backbone of civilization"; i.e., the *family*. In fact, it is quickly being re-defined and eroding.

Pope John Paul II has been clear and outspoken on the Church's support of the mother in the home:

> "It is she, in an extraordinary way because of her motherhood, a bodily as well as spiritual reality, who lavishes love, affection, and care on her children. By nature, she is suited for this. A father's love is not expressed in nearly such an intense physical, i.e., bodily way. It is necessary then for the mother to be with the children in a physical way and to be physically capable of caring for the children. . . . A mother's role is not only crucial to the family but also to society." ("Apostolic Exhortation on the Family," *Covenant of Love*).

So important does John Paul II see the nurturing of children by the mother in the home that he takes it to what some may see as a radical next step, suggesting financial "grants to mothers" who devote "themselves exclusively to their families."

"The true advancement of women," he emphatically says, "requires that labor should be structured in such a way that women do not have to pay for their advancement by abandoning what is specific to them and at the expense of the family, in which women as mothers have an irreplaceable role."

On the Feast of St. Joseph, March 19, 1995, John Paul II gave further emphasis to the meaning and importance of the woman in the home by dedicating St. Joseph to "**housewives**" as true "artisans of the home" and calling for "recognition of 'maternal tasks, the hard work they require and the need children have for care, love and affection.'"

Quite a contrast to secular, godless standards!

What has happened to the American family? A 1990 report titled "Code Blue," the term used in hospitals to signify a life-threatening emergency, was issued by a panel of educators and physicians, which included former Surgeon General C. Everett Koop, leaders from the American Medical Association, the National Association of State Boards of Education, and others. Its findings:

- A million teen girls get pregnant each year.
- Suicide rate for teens has doubled since 1968, making it the second leading cause of death among adolescents.
- Teen arrests are up 30 percent since 1950.
- Homicide is the leading cause of death among 15 to 19 year-old minority youths.

The Code Blue report concludes; "In every community, we are seeing significant numbers of young people with serious social and emotional problems, the consequences of which range from high suicide attempt rates, (10 percent of boys and 18 percent of girls) to depression and alienation resulting in antisocial behavior, poor school performance, and high dropout rates."

"Two income and single-parent families, changes in

society, and a lack of neighborhood cohesiveness that have 'left many children on their own and more isolated from adults' bear the blame for many of the emotional and physical problems teens face today," the report said.

The situation has only worsened.

Today's culture denies the natural roles of man and woman as God intended, whereby the woman, by her very nature, is the nurturer and caretaker and the man, her provider and protector. Children's needs often come last after mom and dad and the ever illusory "fulfillment" that comes with position and possessions.

But what of the couples for whom a second income is essential? Some suggestions gleaned from other young parents:

• **Pray together** and decide what is needed *now* and what can be postponed. Be careful. Most two-income parents concede "We know we spend more just because it's there."

• **Arrange a support system.** Is there a grandparent, relative or favorite friend who could care for the child when mom's away? A familiar and loving caregiver is *always* the most valuable helpmate to the parent who must work. It offers the child the security and constancy needed.

• **Part-time employment may be all that is needed** to get you "over the hump" and through.

• **At-home employment.** Some mothers are very creative in supplying a second income yet maintaining a full-time presence to spouse and children.

One mother, putting her talents to work, advertises on the local supermarket bulletin boards and takes in sewing and alteration work. Another, is using her degree in cosmetology and has a beauty shop in her basement. A retired teacher is tutoring; a music major teaches piano; a former nurse uses her skills to work part-time at a pro-life crisis pregnancy center; yet another serves as a home health companion to seniors and is encouraged to bring her toddler along on visits. The possibilities are endless!

The good news today is the rising ranks of young couples

who forego a second career and income in order to be open to
the blessings of children and to provide an at-home mom.
"God is never outdone in generosity!"

It is this commitment, on the part of both husband and wife,
that guarantees the child the sense of security, stability, and
love. The message the child receives is not spoken but lived:
"I must be pretty important!"

*"So do not worry, saying, 'What shall we eat?' or 'What
shall we drink?' or 'What shall we wear?' For the pagans run
after all these things, and your heavenly Father knows that you
need them" (Matthew 6:31-32).*

Hawaiian Chicken
(We can dream—can't we?)

1 Jar of Orange or Apricot or Marmalade
1 8 oz. French or Russian Dressing
1 pkg Lipton Onion Soup Mix
1/2 Cup Water or so to thin

Pour over chicken pieces. Bake in oven at 350°. Baste often.
(Yummy—just serve with plenty of napkins.)

CHAPTER 8

Family Dinner—Crucial In An Age Of "Eat On The Run"

"He has granted peace in your borders; with the best of wheat he fills you" (Psalm 147:14).

A story in my local paper reported the decline of "the family dinner," contending that with "dual-income parents, frozen foods, microwave ovens, and a takeout joint on every corner," as well as the growing time constraints on couples and children, "fewer families find time to eat together."

What a shame.

A Roper poll published in 1997, estimates that "slightly more than half of all American families manage to eat together five or more days a week," an 18 percent decline since 1976 when 72 percent of families said they dined together regularly.

The article got me thinking about our own dinner time experiences, and just what is lost by those who, perhaps for no other reason than the sheer *convenience* of "getting it over with," have abandoned the practice of daily family dinners.

But let's be honest. Whether its an "empty nest" couple; two career parents; or households similar to ours, with tots to teens; "family dinners" take *effort* and sometimes real planning.

Speaking from personal experience and as a mom of many, I've lived through the supper hours of trying to serve food and eat dinner while rocking or holding a fussy baby. Then there

are the toddler years, with tantrums, and spilled milk, sometimes a nightly occurrence and something I'm not sure we'll
ever outgrow.

Yet, now that all of our children are school age, we're juggling dinnertime around piano lessons, paper routes, sports
events and teenagers' part-time jobs; not to mention their extracurricular schedules.

The more hectic life becomes, the more we realize the
importance of finding time together. And there is no better way
than sitting down to share a meal.

It's nice to know I'm not alone in my thinking.

In fact, there is a growing list of experts who acknowledge
the importance of family meal sharing:

"Families lose something very important for family life if
they abandon the meal together," says William Doherty, professor of family social science at the University of Minnesota,
who is also a family therapist.

"When the ritual becomes lost, people in a family don't even
think of eating together, even if everyone is around," he said.

Doherty claims that when couples and families have distance
in their relationship or conflict, one of the casualties is the
family dinner. "I look upon the loss of the family meal ritual
as a symptom of a family that's becoming more distant."

The Search Institute, a nationally recognized research group
dedicated to the well-being of children and adolescents,
recently released its own recommendations for youth and
essential character building blocks needed to develop responsible, healthy adults.

Institute Director Peter Benson says, "Whether you're talking about rich kids or poor kids, white kids or kids of color,
there is a general collapse of the developmental infrastructure
that is needed to raise healthy kids" when families no longer
eat together on a regular basis.

Along with limiting television watching and an advocacy of
parents reading to their children, Search urges the establish-
ment of routine meal sharing *as a family every day.*

A Minneapolis *Star-Tribune* (1-24-96) story on family meal

time, reported a growing number of educators and professionals who acknowledge the need for family dinnertime.

On an educational level, Diane Beals, assistant professor of education at Washington University in Missouri, claims that family dinner is essential in teaching children good language and communication skills. Children also learn, she contends, about how the world works and how parents feel about different issues.

So true.

As one of my kids recently asked, "Who are WE voting for this year?" A good question and a great teaching tool on civic responsibility, the privilege of living in a free country, and the difference that one vote can make.

Children are the greatest imitators and they learn more by "osmosis," watching, listening, and immitating parents, than any preaching and teaching we offer. Which means parents should always be on their best behavior, knowing their children are watching and forming their own pattern of behavior.

As a seasoned Mom, I've come to realize that even during the periods when we thought our kids weren't listening or had minds of their own, (you know the kind; they are there, but they're not!) they were picking up our ideas, issues, and interests.

I give the credit to prayer, a heap of Sanctifying Grace, and "osmosis."

Even nutrition experts like Mary Story, an associate professor of public health, claim that the children who eat with their families meet their nutritional needs and have better diets than those who do not.

The presence of a parent and eating together does make a difference.

But more than dining together for the sake of the children, married couples with no children in the home, who forsake the ritual of meal sharing, either because of mandated work schedule differences, or just a bad habit that became routine before they realized it, are *never* as unified as those *making time* to be together.

Every family is unique. Each must pursue a family meal time that fits well with their own schedules and activity. Through trial and a few errors we've developed a few of our own rules. Here's what works well for us:

• **Reserve dinnertime for meals and memories.** Put those heavy financial discussions, stressful problem solving, long lectures, or nagging inquiries aside. Dinner goes down better, is easier to digest, and will build cherished memories if this time together is full of laughter and love.

• **Telephone calls, radios, or TV trays lined in front of the tube are out.** This is the time to hear about family happenings. Unless it's an emergency, it can wait. Top priority is each other.

• **No separate eating unless necessary.** Of course, this rule bends when employment, school, extracurricular activities, or special occasions occur, but our family must always feel that these are the exceptions and not the rule.

If you're "Empty Nesters" or a "Two-Career Couple," and solo dining became the norm for convenience more than choice, sit down with your spouse and work out the days and times when you can share meals together and then make every effort to do it.

• **Make dinnertime something to look forward to, even if the meal is little more than leftovers from cleaning out the refrigerator.** The leisure, laughter, and love will be remembered far longer than the menu.

• **Dinnertime may be the first haven of refuge and relief for those who left home in the morning to tackle school, jobs, pressures, and peers.** Make the most of it.

• **Every meal begins with prayer**. Everything tastes better and the conversation is guaranteed more peaceful, spilled milk and all. Truly food and family are gifts from a generous God.

• **Sunday meals are special.** This is the one day of the week that our adult out-of-home and/or married children have a standing invitation to come for dinner (unless we're busy). They love coming home, bringing along grandchildren, dates, or friends. Each of us looks forward to hearing about the goings on of the others. And the fun continues with card playing, board games, and watching old movies to top off the evening.

In our household, Sunday dinners may routinely number fourteen to twenty people. Yes, it's busy and it does involve work. Yet, it's nothing short of a joyful coming together, truly a labor of love, and so vital in nourishing family life.

Throughout Scripture, Christ used food and meal-sharing to demonstrate His love. It was no coincidence that Jesus began His public ministry and performed His first miracle at a banquet, the Marriage Feast at Cana.

It was also at dinner that Christ called Matthew, a despised tax collector, to be one of His apostles and forgave Mary Magdalene. There's room at God's table for every repentant sinner.

Most importantly, The Last Supper, the very first Sacrifice of the Mass, was chosen by Christ as the one and ONLY means to be used by His Church to pass on His REAL presence through the consecrated Bread and Wine.

Family mealtime offers a wonderful and built-in opportunity for parents. Christ calls us to make these occasions a time of relaxation, faith-sharing, and togetherness. Occasionally you may notice, as we have, your own little miracle of healing, forgiveness, understanding, and love.

It may not always be perfect, but if we try to give it focus and priority, God will give us the grace to help solve all those other things which may threaten to undermine the most precious gifts He has bestowed on us, each other.

"The righteous eat to their hearts' content, but the stomach of the wicked goes hungry" (*Proverbs* 13:25).

Grandma K's Hamburger Stroganoff
Another lazy way to make a delicious meal

1 lb Hamburger   1 large Onion
2-3 Celery Stalks   Worcestershire Sauce—shake to taste
Mushrooms (Unless your kids don't like them. Cook separately
   and then serve to *just the adults*.)
1 Can Cream Mushroom Soup
1/2 Can Water
1/2 Pint Sour Cream
1 pkg Wide Egg Noodles (or whatever concoction of noodles
   you have on hand)
Salt and Pepper to taste

I used to go through all of the work and expense of buying
beef, breading it, and making a gravy base for my Beef
Stroganoff until John's mother taught me this trick. It's really
one of those "no-brainers" that takes very little effort (naturally
the recipe is doubled or tripled at our house) yet it's really a
favorite.

* When Tony comes home from the Army, it's one of his
first requests.

Simply brown the meat. Add onions, celery, and mushrooms. Cook till tender. Add cream of mushroom soup, sour
cream, a shake or two of Worcestershire sauce, and let simmer. Cook the noodles till tender and serve the Stroganoff
over the noodles.

* Note: I don't add a lot of salt to my cooking because
Johnny puts the shaker in front of himself every night and salts
everything *before* he's tasted it. Watching that ritual early on
in our marriage made me realize that I can easily cut down on
salt.

CHAPTER 9

A Bus Full Of Blessings

"Praised be the God and Father of our Lord Jesus Christ, who has bestowed on us in Christ every spiritual blessing in the Heavens!" (*Ephesians* 1:3).

Sometimes the most worthwhile thing a parent can do with a child is not the extravagant, like a trip to Disney World, but the everyday, like the afternoon I spent on a school field trip with my son Joseph, and his first grade class.

Did I like riding the big orange bus crammed three to a seat with six-year olds? **No.** Or the volume of noise that seemed to escalate by the mile? Hardly. Or the fact that I could concentrate on little else than the five hyper youngsters I was assigned to watch. "In your dreams," as my kids would say.

What was apparent from the moment I walked into my son's classroom before the trip, was what my coming on this outing meant to Joe. He was thrilled.

I'm a *seasoned* Mom and at one time or another I've played chaperone for all twelve of Joe's older brothers and sisters, joining in field trips, both scenic and scientific; as well as hay rides, sleigh rides, and overnites.

To my recollection, while most of Joe's older siblings expressed great desire in having me come along on their outings; when I did, I received little more than an embarrassed smile or nod from them. After all "someone might see." Yet in my mind, there was little doubt about how much it meant.

Joseph, by contrast, was far from shy at expressing his joy. He held my hand in the lineup, a must with first graders; showed me off to classmates; pulled me back in his range when I appeared too interested in something other than him (never mind the new History Museum, I can see that *any* time); and kissed me sweetly on the bus in front of his seatmate and buddy, Stephen.

To Joseph, mom was along for this school excursion "and that made it perfect," as he later bragged to the family at dinnertime that evening.

I won't be able to go on all of Joseph's field trips, but attending this one was a tender reminder of the bond still fragile and sensitive that is present between small children and their parents.

To infants, preschoolers, and young children like Joseph, "all is okay" when they are reassured and secure by the presence of a parent in the face of a new or strange environment.

My afternoon with Joe's scheduled field trip meant setting aside other plans. Such important stuff, I can't remember what it was. I do know my being there meant *everything* to Joseph. Reason enough for me.

Every psychologist agrees that the first five years of a child's life are the most important and most sensitive. Many an American leader and presidents from Garfield to Reagan, has proclaimed children to be "our greatest natural resource"— our very future.

More importantly, Pope John Paul II, declaring families to be the "Domestic Church," devoted an entire Encyclical, *Letter to Families* in which he reminds the world that "Every individual born and raised in a family constitutes a treasure."

The Holy Father says parents are the "first and most important educators of their children" by their word and their witness. Yet, he says that the very nature of parenthood will "in turn" educate parents by what he calls a "process of exchange": "While they (parents) are teachers of humanity for their own children, they learn humanity *from them*." (My emphasis)

Yep. And I'm, still learning!

I wasn't the only parent riding the yellow bus that day. It was loaded with dads, moms, and even a grandmother to chaperone and escort. One particular grandmother, with a story all her own, was taking the place of her daughter who died suddenly from illness in her twenties, leaving the youngster with no mother. Now that's LOVE!

I thought of all the times when I couldn't go along on such excursions, and of the many who generously watch over our young when we are unable.

Today there is so much talk of status and success; all the while the world grows ever more hungry for the true meaning of happiness.

As Christians we know it comes not from wealth and ownership of *things,* but from the closeness and affection that comes *only* with love! And God is that love.

I believe He tries in a million different ways each day, to show us His love, the true meaning of life. Sometimes those little glimpses of Heaven come in very small forms.

Like the day I rode the big yellow bus with one of those "treasures" who wanted me along for the ride!

"Yes, in joy you shall depart, in peace you shall be brought back; Mountains and hills shall break out in song before you, and all the trees of the countryside shall clap their hands" (*Isaiah* 55:12).

Open-Faced Veggie Sandwiches
For that impromptu lunch or drop-in guest, or when
the frig. or cupboard is bare.

Bread Slices, wheat or white
Onions, chopped fine
Salad Dressing, Ranch, Creamy Cucumber
Cucumber, chopped small
Sour Cream, (if you have no salad dressing)
Tomatoes, diced
Celery, chopped
Broccoli, chopped
Mushrooms or Blk Olives, chopped
Zucchini or whatever you have
Carrots, shredded
Cheese, shredded, Cheddar or Swiss

   Lay the bread slices on a flat jelly roll pan and cover with
salad dressing. Then sprinkle the shredded or diced vegetables
on top. Don't be afraid to pile it high. Cover the top with the
Swiss or cheddar cheese (I do some with cheddar and some
with Swiss. This way your guests have a choice and it looks
like you've fussed a bit more than just cleaning out your frig.
and tossing it together.) Bake in slow (250°) oven and serve
when cheese has melted over the top. Serve with sour cream
dip, chips, relishes, and soup if desired.

CHAPTER 10

The Mere Intent To Pray Is A Prayer

"Life is more important than food and the body more than clothing. Consider the ravens: they do not sow, they do not reap, they have neither cellar nor barn—yet God feeds them. How much more important you are than the birds! Which of you by worrying can add a moment to his life-span? If the smallest things are beyond your power why be anxious about the rest?" (Luke 12:23-26).

"A penny for your thoughts" my mother used to say, whenever she wanted to know what was on our minds.

In my own case, it almost always opened me up and got me talking. (I suppose my friends might say, "It doesn't take much.")

It wasn't the "penny" but the invitation that often broke the ice. There were more than a few times when I might not have talked over a concern at all had Mom not asked. Smart Mom.

When it comes to parenting, I believe the same logic or incentive can be used when teaching our children to pray. Not that we offer them pennies or bribery, but that we encourage them to think about offering their prayer intentions aloud during family prayer.

Every time intentions are voiced in this active family, the prayer takes on a special meaning and seems to come alive.

45

And, of course, in this household of little ones, we've learned from experience that it can include *everything* from the seemingly silly to the serious and sacred.

"Dear Jesus, help them *git* the warts off my hands and make it not hurt so bad," six-year-old Joseph whispered the night before he was to have outpatient care for the more than half dozen eruptions on his little hands and feet. (He was convinced "it was from catching so many toads at the cabin" but that's another prayer.) We all smiled and prayed.

The night before John was to go in for a more serious surgery, our family knelt to pray the Rosary. It was too solemn and downright scarey for some of our young. Afterward, we each took holy water and gently placed it on John's forehead. As the holy water dripped down his face, we all broke into laughter at the sight, temporarily forgetting our concerns, and realizing that God was in charge. And, indeed, He was. All was okay.

Sometimes our children vocalize a prayer or concern that we had no idea was on their mind. It helps us join them in prayer and in some instances, to talk about what we can do to help.

"Science is *hard*—and my project is a mess!" our seventh grader blurted out one evening during prayers. Organizing and punctuality were not his forte, but after prayertime, his brothers and sisters moved in with their own set of suggestions and opinions. He was off and running from there. Prayer works.

Next is the part so often neglected by most of us: "Thanking God" for answered prayers, prayers of thanksgiving.

"How often do we hand the Lord our list of grievances or 'gimmies,' give me this or give me that, and then forget to go back and say thank you when He has answered our prayers?" I ask my children.

The practice of praying aloud for friends, loved ones, or specific interests, not only helps us remain focused and to really think about the needs of others as well as our own, but it also helps us to remember to be thankful and to express that gratitude in prayer.

On more than a few occasions, it is *the kids* who remind me:

"Hey Mom, remember last week when we prayed about Michael's allergies, and now he's so much better?"

Sometimes our thanksgiving prayers have been unsolicited and spontaneous. Such as the time we were driving through Nebraska and were caught on the freeway in a ferocious thunder and hailstorm. We pulled off the road and prayed all the while the car swayed from the angry wind and white hailstones that repeatedly battered the top of our van. It seemed like an eternity until it subsided and when it finally did our cheers went up simultaneously: "Thank you Jesus!"

Only when we proceeded to the next town and saw the homes and yards with debris from the storm and hundreds of damaged cars that had been dented and pitted by baseball sized hail, did we realize that had we traveled farther, we would have been in the center of something far worse.

I like vocalizing prayer intentions because it cuts down on distraction and helps us remain focused, giving special meaning to each prayer.

"Most of us become distracted when we pray," I tell my kids, "but do not be discouraged! Saint Augustine says, 'The mere *intent* to pray is a prayer.' You can't beat that for answered prayers."

We want our children to know that God knows what is in our hearts and perhaps on our minds, even when we forget or our attention wanders. If we *intend* to make a certain action or prayer a special focus, then no matter what, it still becomes a prayer. The trick is our *intention* or will.

Family prayer time only improves when we share those special intentions aloud with others. In fact, we've gotten into the habit of dedicating individual mysteries when we say the evening Rosary. It helps keep our attention and reminds us of those in need of our prayers.

Jesus was very clear about the power of praying together, telling us *". . . if two of you join your voices on earth to pray for anything whatever, it shall be granted you by my Father in heaven. Where two or three are gathered in my name, there am I in their midst"* (*Matthew* 18:19-20).

Of course we want to remind our children that God answers *all* our prayers *in His timing*. And, when He does answer, He gives us only those things that will bring us closer to Him. We can't lose.

My kids will tell you that I cheat because I'll use just about *any* place to offer a little prayer, especially in the car. Yes, I suppose you could say they're a "captive audience," but all of us concede that our car rides, vacations, and even our errands are quieter and calmer (it cuts down on quarrelling) when we remember to take the time to offer some prayers, and especially to ask God's guardian angels for protection and, as I like to say, to "ride the front fenders."

A good opener is: "Who should we pray for today? Does anyone have something or someone on their mind?" It works almost as well as "a penny for your thoughts!"

"O Lord, open my lips, and my mouth shall proclaim your praise" (Psalm 51:17).

Nothin Fancy White Sugar Cookies
This recipe makes the equivalent of a double batch

1 Cup Powdered Sugar	2 tsp Vanilla
1 Cup Granulated Sugar	5 Cups Flour
1 Cup Butter	1 tsp Soda
1 Cup Vegetable Oil	1 tsp Cream of Tartar
2 Eggs (beaten)	1/4 tsp Salt

Combine ingredients. Roll in balls. Press with glass coated with sugar. Bake at 350° for 10 to 12 minutes. These are just old-fashioned sugar cookies but still a hit with everyone at our house.

CHAPTER 11

Taking Time Out

"At every opportunity pray in the Spirit, using prayers and petitions of every sort. Pray constantly and attentively for all in the holy company" (*Ephesians* 6:18).

"If I don't have an intelligent *adult* conversation pretty soon, I think I'll go batty." Sue confided. "Rick and I haven't been out together in months."

"Some days," she continued, "I spend more hours relating to my preschoolers than I do talking to my husband, or for that matter, anyone older than five."

Sue is not alone. For most young mothers today who have set aside their careers to be home with their children, the absence of adult camaraderie in their daily lives is a common dilemma, and often the greatest loss.

"I've been there myself," I told Sue, "and I have John to thank for doing something about it before things became stale."

"So what did you do?"

"Well, it wasn't too many years after we began having children that we found ourselves almost swallowed up by the sheer monotony. Between John's work schedule and my absorption in household responsibilities and kids, our weekends seemed reserved for the big chores, along with grocery shopping, and extended family. We soon were too busy or too tired to take time out for ourselves," I told her.

"That's it exactly!" Sue conceded.

Thankfully, John saw the problem and insisted we *both* needed more time together. "We started *dating* again and that made all the difference in the world."

"Wow!"

"Once we began to set aside a few evenings a month, we found ourselves refreshed and rejuvenated, with *more energy* for family, rather than less. Of course, I occasionally have to remind myself not to use this time to talk about the latest crisis or problem."

"At first it was awkward," I related. "Sometimes I would get a sitter, take the bus downtown and meet John for lunch, and then laughingly begin, 'Lets see now, do I have anything to say if I can't talk about the kids?'"

Soon those lunch dates were filled with talk and renewed affection.

"On those occasions we did use some of those dates to problem-solve a current crisis, there was a closeness and calmness in knowing we had taken our time, rather than find ourselves acting in the eye of the tornado."

Perhaps it was nothing more than a Friday night walk to the Dairy Queen, dinner at a nearby pizza parlor, taking in a band concert in the park, or going for a bike ride or stroll around the lake. (In Minnesota we're fortunate to be loaded with wonderful lakes and parks.) All these cheap dates kept us in tune and in touch with each other.

"It doesn't have to be fancy just relaxing," I told Sue.

But I learned something else in those early, at-home mothering years. In addition to my need for John's love and companionship, I was beginning to miss something pretty vital to most average women—the camaraderie and just plain "girl talk" that comes with friendship and the good conversation of others.

While most men get along, rarely feeling a need for small talk or deep conversation, women are social beings and crave those "heart-to-hearts" that seem to add meaning and depth to their lives. Maintaining close friendships with others is one of the more obvious solutions to isolation and boredom. Choosing friends who share our faith and fundamental values is also certain to strengthen supportive ties.

"One of my favorite things to look forward to is lunch with a girlfriend or an afternoon of shopping, just to see what's in and fashionable," I told Sue.

"But what do you do with the kids?" Sue asked.

"This is where having Grandma, a sister, close friend, or neighbor really helps. Offering a stay-at-home mom a little 'R and R' (rest and relaxation) is, in my view, a Corporal Work of Mercy!" I told Sue. "Some gals have gotten pretty creative in helping each other by taking turns babysitting for those 'time outs.'"

Joining a women's group at church is another means of socialization and is *always* a good idea. It not only introduces us to acquaintances and new friends, but involves us in issues and interests outside of ourselves. As that happens and we take on other concerns, we become more interesting.

Another way is volunteering. With so many women working full-time outside the home, there is a real shortage of help in hospitals, nursing homes, emergency food centers, meals on wheels, etc. Sharing their time and talent in these areas, serving in the pro-life movement, or working as an aid at their child's school has been fulfilling and rewarding for millions of moms.

While this may not always be possible for the new or breast-feeding mother, or those with small preschoolers, some women have become downright clever about juggling schedules in order to maintain a connection with the volunteer work they feel so vital.

"The volunteers we rely on are professional and caring in their work," a hospital administrator and friend recently stated. "Still, many tell us they go back home to their families feeling even more renewed and committed after spending time helping others." I know the feeling. As a volunteer counselor at a local pro-life crisis pregnancy center, I've often felt *I'm the one who is benefiting* and not those we serve.

But, still there is another dimension to the needs of the at-home mother: the spiritual element which is a part of each of us. Of course there are at-home study groups formed parish-by-parish, in addition to exciting new programs such as Familia or the Apostolate of Family Consecration. However, some women may need something a bit more informal and requiring less commitment.

When my daughter, Chrissy, and her husband had their first baby, Elizabeth, she quit her teaching position to become a full-time homemaker and mommy. Her complaint was the same: "My neighborhood is like a ghost town during the day. There's just no one around to even talk to, except for Esther, who is a real sweetheart, but at eighty-four we don't have a lot in common."

Chrissy wasted little time doing something about it. First, she called a few close friends in her parish and talked to them about coming to her home for a weekly prayer and social hour. Everyone she called jumped at the invitation.

"Next, I got real brave," she recalls. "I began contacting some others, gals I really didn't know very well but thought they just might be interested. 'What have I got to lose' I asked myself, and that got me over any shyness or hesitation.

"The response was terrific! Everyone loved the idea of beginning with the Rosary, keeping in mind any special intentions of the group, and then using the remainder of the time for coffee, goodies, and just plain girl talk!"

Since those first weeks, Chrissy's small group of women has steadily grown, with new moms who come for prayer and friendship.

And the bonus? Some of the women, including a few who were raised Catholic, were unfamiliar with the Rosary or group prayer. It didn't take long and they were leading decades and eagerly sharing prayer requests.

Another surprise? A couple of newcomers were not Catholic but, as one young woman told Chrissy, "I really enjoy the Rosary and prayertime and I feel welcome by the openess of the group."

Hmmm. A whole new idea in ecumenism and evangelization. And to think it all began with the notion of "Taking Time Out!"

"Again I tell you if two of you join your voices on earth to pray for anything whatever, it shall be granted you by my Father in heaven. Where two or three are gathered in my name, there am I in their midst" (Matthew 18:19-20).

Grandma D's *French Silk Pie*
This one is better than pie shops

1/2 Cup Butter (use real butter)
3/4 Cup Sugar
1 Sq Unsweetened Chocolate (melted)
1 tsp Vanilla
2 Eggs
1 Pie Shell (9-inch)

Hint: I double this recipe for a 9 or 10 inch pie. It leaves a little left over but the pie doesn't look skimpy.

Cream butter—adding sugar gradually. Cream *well.* Add chocolate and vanilla and blend well. Add eggs one at a time beating each egg *five* minutes (this is a must—5 minutes each). Then turn into prepared pie shell. Chill and top with whipped cream.

* This one came from my mother. It is *super* rich and delicious. My gang looks forward to it at Christmas and can sometimes con me into making it on other holidays.

CHAPTER 12

Keeping Sleep-Overs Special And Fun

"The Lord is your guardian; the Lord is your shade; he is beside you at your right hand. The sun shall not harm you by day, nor the moon by night. The Lord will guard you from all evil" (*Psalm* 121:5-6).

"What do you do about sleep-overs?" asked Jean, a young mother of three.

"Our Megan is in the third grade and I'm already hearing about "birthday sleep-overs." It's just a matter of time before we face the issue and I'm not feeling very comfortable about the idea.

With good reason.

Jean's instincts about over-nights for young children are not misplaced. Many a parent when faced with the issue find themselves weighing the pros and cons, after all they *are* fun, and perhaps asking a more experienced mom "What's a good rule of thumb or proper age?"

Most moms remember the fun times had at what we called "pajama parties" or sleep-overs. Whether an evening with one special friend, or the more rowdy occasions when a whole group of girls stayed over-night together, it was an exhaustive event full of music, movies, game playing, snacks, and endless hours of girl talk and giggles.

The same holds true for today's youth, with two exceptions: 1. Young boys are now into sleep-over parties, and 2. Such events are no longer reserved for young teens but can actually begin as early as third grade.

And there's the rub!

Just because a young child asks to sleep at a friend's house doesn't necessarily mean she/he is mature enough, or has any idea what being away *all* night from home and family is really like.

This hit home the first time we gave in to the pleadings of our daughter who begged and begged for her little school friend to "stay overnight so we can play games and talk." We knew Suzie well and she had been to our home on many occasions. The girls were young in age, but because of the closeness of their friendship, we saw no problem.

Wrong!

All was fine and the girls were perfectly pleased, eating their pizza, playing board games, laughing and chatting. Until that is, the evening wore on, darkness covered the windows, and the house became lifeless as everyone else bedded down.

By midnight I was on the phone calling Suzie's mother. Now in tears, she'd changed her mind. "Suzie wants to come home." I told her half-asleep mom.

And so, my husband John, slipped his top coat over his pajamas and padded in his slippers to the garage and cold car, to drive little Suzie safely home to her waiting parents, where she could then fall securely asleep.

From then on, no more "all nights" for little ones.

For most parents like us, all it takes is one late-night "Suzie episode," or watching a child sleepy-eyed, crabby, and dragging, through the "day after the night before," to realize that endurance parties or night-overs are too intense for small children.

We may sometimes be the only parents who say "No." And, we may not always be *popular*, but John and I would rather be careful and cautious than having to drive a frightened youngster home in the middle of the night.

"There's a good reason why toddlers and young children sometimes climb into their parents bed at night or early in the morning," I told Jean. "It's called reassurance. They simply need to know we're close by."

As for the boys: While we do permit over-nights with a special buddy or two during the summer or holidays, we've learned to be fairly cautious about *group parties.*

Why the difference?

Well, certainly girls can be nearly as noisy with their music, loud giggles, and screeching. Most, however, do settle down as the evening wears on and are content to spend the hours giggling, talking fashion, gossip, and girl talk. Females crave companionship, socialization, and the friendship that evolves from conversational sharing.

Boys, on the other hand, express their loyalty, not by lengthy dialogues or emotional exchanges, but by shared interests in doing; be it building projects, creative technology, art, or most commonly, team sports.

"Males are more physical and their concept of *party* is always a bit wilder," Pat, one of my wiser mentors warned me. Casual chatter, fun conversation, and even competitive games such as board, computer, or backyard hoops and ball can easily give way to punching contests, "war games," or fights whenever there are multiple personalities and hours of unstructured time involved.

Proof was the night our Michael, an eleven-year-old who had previously begged to stay all night with his buddies for a classmate's birthday sleep-over, poured his tired body in the front seat and confessed, "I guess I'm not sorry to leave. It was getting wild and a couple guys left the party to go fight some other kids down the street. I *knew* that wasn't a good idea!"

Thank heavens!

As a mom of many, and through our own trial and error, we've come up with the following guidelines for sleep-overs that work well and lessen the chance of tired and cranky kids, or another "Suzie episode":

• No all-night parties are allowed for young, elementary-aged children (under ten). It's too exhausting and small children still need the security, privacy, and reassurance of their own parents close at hand.

• No sleep-overs during the school year even on weekends for grade-school aged children. The only exception *may* be during Christmas or Easter/Spring Holidays. And even then, there are **no group sleep-overs**.

• No over-nights or parties allowed unless one or both parents are home. Unfortunately, some folks use such occasions as pacifiers or companion-sitters for their children while they are at work or out for an evening. A bad idea which is fraught with potential danger.

• Know the children your child is with and *always* get phone numbers and addresses. If you've never met the parents, a quick and friendly call goes a long way in easing your mind.

• Regarding parties that combine birthdays and sleep-overs, we've come up with a workable *compromise:* The child may attend the birthday party and stay later than usual (we call that curfew bending), but when ten or ten-thirty (depending upon the age) comes around, we're there to pick them up and bring them home.

What's interesting about this is that in almost *every* instance, our child was more than ready to come home and settle down.

"I don't mind leaving. I was getting bored and tired," our seventh grade Kari once confided on the drive home after one such eagerly awaited evening.

• Ration the over-nights no matter the age. Whether with one friend or many, teens and high schoolers especially require sleep. Not less sleep—but more. All night parties are tiring and sap their much-needed energy. Remember, sleep-overs have little to do with sleep or rest.

• Don't give in to every over-night request even for older teens. Keep in mind, the following day will be spent trying to make up for the lost sleep.

• No co-ed camping or over-nights no matter the age. You may think this will never be an issue at your house, but if you are a parent in today's world, it will come up. Your high-school or college-age young adult may be invited to such functions and this is where Christian parents must be very clear in telling them: "Not an option, as long as you live here." They may not realize that this can cause scandal to others; jeopardizes the reputations of everyone involved; is an occasion of sin because of the surrounding temptations; and most importantly with little privacy, no chaperones or safeguards, there is absolutely NO guarantee about what could happen. Even with the best of kids. All it takes is the added influence of alcohol, illegal drugs, or the irresistible influence of another.

• Remember children, even young adults, depend on parents to set standards and to warn them about events or entanglements we know to be "powder kegs" or just plain wrong. After all, that's what being a parent is all about.

Sleep-overs or no, we want our children to know that we *and* their Guardian Angel are close by them.

"When you lie down, you need not be afraid, when you rest, your sleep will be sweet" (*Proverbs* 3:24).

Baked Egg Dish
This dish will feed a whole crowd—
for breakfast or brunch

(Prepare the night before)

12 Eggs
1/2 lb Bacon
12 oz grated Cheddar Cheese
1/2 tsp Salt
1/8 tsp Pepper
1 1/4 Cup Milk
10 slices of plain white bread (don't try fancy, it won't work)

Fry bacon and drain off fat. Grease large cake pan with salad oil or bacon drippings. Trim crusts from about 10 slices of bread. (Cheap light commercial. Homemade doesn't work well.) Line bottom of pan with bread slices and fill in any spaces with part slices. Sprinkle with grated cheese (I like to combine with Swiss or varied kinds) and bacon pieces. Mix together eggs, salt and pepper, and milk. Pour over top, cover, and refrigerate overnight.

Bake at 250° for 1 hour. Test center with clean knife till knife comes out clean. If not done, raise temp to 350° after first hour.

(* This test doesn't always work for me because I load it with so much cheese and extras. Just watch for puffy middle—no soggy bottom.)

Options to add: onions, broccoli, ham, sausage, shredded carrots, tomatoes, mushrooms, varied cheeses. Mmmmmmmm. (It all depends on what your kids will let you get by with. Sometimes I just dress up a corner or half for us "big folks.")

* This recipe came from a mother of 16 children! A woman after my own heart.

CHAPTER 13

Praying For Our Kids

"Your Heavenly Father knows all that you need. Seek first His kingship over you, His way of holiness and all these things will be given you besides"(Matthew 6:32-33).

Perhaps the greatest thing we can do for our children besides pray for them is to *tell* them we're praying.

There is a powerful and persuasive force that goes into action when we witness to our faith. And what better witness to our own young than letting them know who and what we pray for. Especially, when it is *they* who are the focus of our prayers.

I remember the first time I told one of my rebellious teens, "I'm praying for you. We raised you to know right from wrong and now I pray that when the temptations come up, you'll make the right decision."

"Oh Great!" he responded. "What chance does a guy have?"

"None," I quickly assured him. "I use every weapon I have to protect you from something that could ruin your life or harm your soul."

It may not prevent our young from succumbing to sin or bad judgment decisions altogether; after all, there is such a thing as *free will;* but what it does do is remind them that our love and desire for their well being is so paramount, we look to God Himself to insure their happiness.

The *Catechism of the Catholic Church* reminds us that, "The

Christian Family is the first place of education in prayer. Based on the Sacrament of Marriage, the family is the "domestic church" where God's children learn to pray "as the Church" and to persevere in prayer. For young children in particular, daily family prayer is the first witness of the Church's living memory as awakened patiently by the Holy Spirit."

In our large and diverse household, we need all the "awakening" we can muster.

Make no mistake, we couldn't do this without prayer. In fact, having these kids has strengthened our faith, brought us closer to God and to each other, and enriched our prayer life as never before.

No matter the challenges (and that we've had!) and regardless of our cultural differences or diversity, it was the prayer that held us together, kept us together, and, in a few situations, brought the wayward home.

The Church teaches that God will give us all the grace and tools parents need to guide their young. **But the grace and tools will *only* come if we stay close to the church and ask God for help. And the way we ask is by talking to Him in prayer.**

For nearly eleven years I belonged to a prayer group which met weekly in my home. Though my school-aged children never attended, they *knew* this Wednesday morning group of pray-ers could do a number on just about any form of evil the Devil threw at them.

We saw answered prayers for everything from minor medical to handicapping disabilities. In cases of the heart, we saw adolescents to young adults turn from entanglements with belligerence, drugs, gambling, fornication, adultery, divorce, and you-name-it. It may have taken months or years, but the majority of those we prayed for came back to their family and back to their faith. This experience taught me patience and perseverance in my prayer life.

I also learned there's truth to the old adage, "If there's a parent out there praying for you, give it up. No use trying to live a life of sin and debauchery when someone's praying!"

Yet, many parents cannot rely on groups or the prayers of others. That's where the Holy Spirit comes in. The *Catechism* tells us that "prayer comes also from the Holy Spirit" and not from ourselves alone.

The Holy Spirit is a part of each prayer we utter and actually prays *with* us for our needs. How's that for power!

According to the *Catechism*, prayer is also *mystery.* "Some see prayer as a flight from the world in reaction against activism; but in fact, Christian prayer is neither an escape from reality nor a divorce from life."

Thus, we want to remind our children *often,* not just when they're in trouble, of the power that comes with prayer.

As my Michael recently asked, "Mom, were you praying for me today? I did so well on the test, I figured you must have prayed for me!"

That's the way I want my kids to remember me, urging their success and well-being even when I'm not there in person.

It's also the best way to encourage our children to rely on prayer in every situation they face. One of my favorite prayers is to offer up the daily chores and tasks that I do for my children. **Thus, every floor I sweep and dish I wash becomes a prayer to God on behalf of one of my sons or daughters. I may not always think to do it, but when I do, my work becomes easier and my worry-load lighter.**

Maybe that's where the phrase *"Domestic Church,"* comes from.

What's fun is to see the expression on a face when I occasionally say, "Well Mikey, today was your day and I offered up my laundry and housework just for you. So, I expect to see *great* things from you kid!" It always brings a smile.

The *Catechism* tells us, *"It is always possible to pray.* (Their emphasis.). . . It is possible to offer fervent prayer even while walking in public or strolling alone, or seated in your shop. . . while buying or selling. . . or even while cooking."

That's me! I'm usually in the kitchen and if it's not the cooking, it's the cleaning. The real trick in all this is *remembering.*

A helpmate is to start each day with the Morning Offering, *intending* to make all of our "prayers, works, joys, and sufferings" a gift to God. When we do that, it will be! The trick is *intending* it as a prayer.

Perhaps the kindest, most compassionate thing we can do for one of our wayward children is not to shrug and say, "Well, it's your decision and your life." Strangers do that! Rather, we must tell them of their error and let them know we are praying.

A twenty-two-year-old woman, pregnant and unmarried, confided to a pro-life counselor of her original intent to have an abortion. "I was raised Catholic, but when I told my parents of my pregnancy they said the decision was all mine and they'd support me in whatever I chose to do. I scheduled myself for an abortion because I thought if it didn't make that much difference to them what I did, I might as well take the easy way out. I changed my mind after seeing the pro-life billboard and hotline number. I just couldn't go through with it."

Here is a lesson learned to tell parents of all ages. Love your young enough to tell them right from wrong! Does it guarantee an end to rebellion? No. I remember one particular kid who snapped back with a sharp, "Don't bother!" when I told him I was praying for him.

This is the same son, a few years later, who asks for prayers before final exams, job interviews, or moving decisions. Funny what a few years of maturity can do.

Step number one is to Instruct the Ignorant (if they don't know); Counsel the Doubtful (if they are open to your message); and, when all else fails, to Admonish the Sinner. A child, *no matter the age*, must be told his or her actions are destructive and sinful. As parents we have a unique opportunity and responsibility to remind our young of God's laws, His forgiveness, and His love. Let's remember that to admonish sin is a Spiritual Work of Mercy and God will bless our effort even when it appears futile.

As one of my friends told her daughter who defiantly announced her decision to live with her boyfriend, "I do not approve of the way you are living your life and I'll have no part in supporting it in any way. But it doesn't change the fact that I'll always love you. *And, I'm going to pray* that you'll stop and do the right thing. It's never too late for chastity!"

Step number two is to pray. Temptation is a serious thing. Most of us parents have more than a vivid memory. It always comes disguised as attractive, alluring, and fun. Sin chips away at our will power, attacks our weakest area, and is habit forming.

St. Paul repeatedly reminds us to *"Rejoice always, never cease praying, render constant thanks such is God's will for you in Christ Jesus"* (*1 Thessalonians* 5:16).

He also reminds us of the power of the Holy Spirit and the saints, pray at all times in the Spirit, with all prayer and supplication. To that end keep alert with all perseverence making supplication for all the saints.

I recently met a young woman who told of her previous abortion and fifteen-year separation from the Catholic faith. "I immediately distanced myself from my family and friends. It caused the breakup of my marriage and there is no question that my rejection of the Church and my choosing a militant feminist lifestyle and pro-abortion activism was to cover the guilt I had over the baby I aborted."

"I sincerely believe that **the only reason I am here today, my relationship to my family and my faith restored, is because I have a mother and family who never quit praying for me.**"

Somehow through all the years, the sin, and the separation, the love of faith and family prevailed. Prayer is powerful!

Catholic parents have a whole arsenal of saints to pray to, to lean on, and to tell our kids about. We also have a common union of saints to pray along with us. That's what's meant by the "Communion of Saints."

My Angela, then a bright thirteen-year-old, came bounding in the door from school one day and announced, "There were only three of us in the entire seventh grade who knew the Guardian Angel and St. Michael the Archangel prayers. Gosh,

I thought everyone knew those prayers!"

And this is at a traditional Catholic school, yet it is not surprising in this secular age. Religious education, however, is
meant to be a **secondary** reinforcement of our faith and
morals. It is the parents who are the **primary** educators and,
as my pastor likes to say, the *"first missionaries"* to their children. Thank heavens God provides lots of help.

The Guardian Angel prayer and prayer to St. Michael the
Archangel, who is said to be God's most powerful warrior, are
two prayers that can arm us and our children for the daily
temptations that threaten their spiritual well-being.

When one of my young adults left home, not on the best of
terms, to "do his own thing," I prayed daily to *his* guardian
angel, his patron saint, and The Blessed Mother to watch over
and protect him.

And when he returned months later, ready to buckle down
and asking for a second chance, I knew who to thank for praying with me.

Often through my parenting years and especially in raising
healthy teens, I've looked to the saints, such as: St. Maria
Goretti (Patron Saint of Chastity), St. Joseph (Patron of the
Family), St. Anthony of Padua (Patron of Lost Articles—also
works for "lost" kids!), my children's patron saints, and their
guardian angels.

But the one I lean on most, who I depend on to hear my
prayers, plead my case, and console my impatient heart is
Mary. She is our Mother and who, more than Mary, would
have her Son's ear? And who more than Mary can understand
our fears, pains, needs, and desires as a parent?

In that regard, I've come to rely on the Rosary and in each
one that I pray, my children are always somewhere in those
beads! I also know that my parenting has been richly strengthened since I began attending daily Mass. There is no greater
prayer than the Mass.

Have all my prayers been answered? Yes, every one of them.
Answered in the way I wanted? No. When things happen not
according to *my* will, I have learned through the years that if

I let go and let God, *"all things will work together for good for those who love the Lord,"* as St. Paul so beautifully reminds us.

After all, our children are only on loan to us from a Heavenly Father who loves them far more than we have the capacity to even imagine. If we want their happiness and well-being, God wants it more. Not just on earth but for all eternity.

Skeptics may still say that "all of this is well and good," but what about the tough nuts to crack? What about those children who don't seem to show improvement in spite of our saintly pleadings or persistent praying? Worse still, are the young adults who have chosen a way of life that jeopardizes their very soul because of an insistence to use and abuse chemicals, alcohol, gambling, sex, or others.

A great test of faith, trust and *patience in God's timing!* Yes, I've been there.

As difficult as that may be, our faith teaches us that God our Father loves our children far more than we do and that every prayer we utter on their behalf will **not** go unheeded.

Whenever I have a particularly stubborn prayer request that continues to go unanswered, I think of my Aunt Dolores. Aunt Dolores was a member of our prayer group and every Wednesday, she offered the same plea, "And for my son, Ted, Lord. Please help him straighten up his life and come back to the Church."

All of us, witnessing the anguish in this dear woman's face over a ten-year period, prayed it would happen. The hurt she bore as a result of her son's estrangement made us all want to pray for his rejection of alcohol and return to the Church.

It didn't happen. Dolores died never seeing the answer she so desperately sought. Yet, her faith never wavered. It only increased. In fact, I believe Aunt Dolores' bedrock belief gave courage and strength to all who knew her and witnessed her unwavering love of God.

Aunt Dolores taught me trust. We may not see the results we want in this world, but if we let go and let God, our prayers *will* be heard.

Yes, our children will be confronted with occasions of sin and obstacles to their faith. But, they have us and we have the answer. The answer is Jesus. And He assures us that all we need do is ask. That's what praying for our kids is all about, isn't it?

Here's some tips we've used in talking to our children about prayer:

• Tell your children you are praying for them. Never assume. Tell them: "I love you. I'm praying for you."

• Tell your children: "I expect great things from you because God loves you and will give you all the help you need. Just ask Him."

• Pray to your children's Guardian Angel and to St. Michael the Archangel.

• Teach your children the Guardian Angel and St. Michael prayers. These are more than lovely prayers they are weapons against evil!

• Offer up your daily chores and tasks as a prayer for your child.

• Go to Mass often for your young. More than once a week if you can.

• Pray the Rosary. The Blessed Mother wants to pray with us. Ask her help.

• Trust Jesus. We don't need to see results we'll see them later.

"Know that the Lord does wonders for his faithful one; the Lord will hear me when I call upon him" (*Psalm* 4:4).

Oatmeal Raisin Cookies
Mary Elizabeth's Specialty

1 Cup Shortening (I use half Butter or Margarine
1 Cup Brown Sugar
1 Granulated Sugar
2 Eggs
1 tsp Vanilla
1 1/2 Cups Flour
1 tsp Salt
1 tsp Soda
3 Cups Oatmeal
1 Cup Raisins
1/2 Cup Walnuts (chopped)

Cream together shortening and sugars; beat in eggs and vanilla. Sift together flour, salt, and soda. Stir into creamed mixture. Stir in oats, raisins, and nuts. Form into small balls; place about 1 1/2 inches apart on greased cookie sheet. Bake at 350° about 10 minutes or until lightly brown. Cool slightly before removing to cooling rack. Makes about 6 dozen.

* Mary Elizabeth leaves the nuts out because she doesn't like nuts in cookies. They're still delicious cookies.

CHAPTER 14

"Occasions Of Sin" And "Angels In Disguise"

"The eyes of the Lord are in every place, keeping watch on the evil and the good" (*Proverbs* 15:3).

I sometimes think that if the kids of today just had one busybody relative or interfering grandmother, godmother, uncle or aunt, someone who minced no words when it came to telling them about the difference between right and wrong and how God calls them to live, they would be far better off. And there sure would be less confusion and mixed messages.

Imagine if every time a kid were on the brink of getting into trouble, there'd be another adult to echo a parent's message, "Stay clear of that. It could mess up your life!"

I wish more people were like the grandmother I met in Iowa. "I'm such a busybody," she confided. "I'm always sending my grandchildren information on our faith, and good items I see that promote chastity and warn about sex outside of marriage and the evils of abortion. I want them to know how I feel!"

I'll bet they know. And, I'll bet they'd hate to disappoint her.

I was reared by a strong German mother and an Italian father who responded with what seemed like guillotine swiftness at the mere hint of impropriety or bad behavior. "You'll do that over my dead body!" was Mom's usual comeback.

Dad, on the other hand, was more worried we'd "grow up

to be bums" or in my case, "marry one!" "What *you* need to
think about," he'd say, "is work. NOT play. Keep busy and
you'll keep outta trouble!"

We were reminded it seemed *often* about 'sin,' confession,
the Ten Commandments (yes, we broke them), and that phrase
(that seems today as extinct as our treasured 33 LP records)
the "occasions of sin."

Yes, "occasions of sin."

Occasions of sin, to us kids growing up, were all those
alleys and avenues we could place ourselves in, which could
"tempt us beyond our control" causing us to commit a sinful
act that we would not otherwise commit.

The *Baltimore Catechism* defined it as, "any person, place,
or thing which may lead us into sin." Somehow we all knew
what that meant.

When Mom or Dad would rattle off the "don'ts" or the
"stay-away-froms" we knew which of those pals or parties
meant "trouble" with a capital T.

"Tell me who you go with and I'll tell you who you are!"
Mom would say. A subtle reminder that if we picked up with
shabby friends, their reputation would soon be ours.

To young girls it might mean an attractive guy who was
known to have "only one thing on his mind." No point in
going on *that* date.

To the boys it meant hanging out with "losers," guys who
seemed to collect trouble for a hobby be it illegal drinking,
drugs, or going with girls they called "easy."

"If the crowd you're with is up to 'no good,'" Mom would
warn, "Don't think you're going to change them. They'll
change you!" And right she was. Everyone knew too about the
"passion pits," what we jokingly labeled the local drive-in
movies or out-of-the-way park spots. Yep, "occasions of sin."

The *Catechism* didn't leave us in the lurch, however. It also
told us how we could keep from committing sin by "prayer,
receiving the sacraments often; by remembering that God is
always with us; by recalling that our bodies are temples of the
Holy Spirit; by keeping occupied with work or play; by

promptly resisting the sources of sin within us; and **by avoiding the near occasions of sin.**" No doubt that's what Dad and Mom had in mind.

Today, when I tell my kids about staying away from "occasions of sin" they roll their eyes and look at each other and grin. I caught a couple whispers under their teenage breaths, "Did she make this one up?"

"Ya mean it's not just good enough to stay away from sin, we have to stay away from anything *near* sin?" one smart-alecky son asked.

"You got it!" I replied. "Stay clear of those areas that can tempt you beyond your control. Use the common sense God gave you and ask your guardian angels to help you."

Here's where surrounding family and friends, in addition to teachers, coaches, and other role models, are so vital to parents and can literally become, as I tell my kids, "angels in disguise."

Who better to help set a wavering kid straight and to tell them the difference between right and wrong than another adult the child looks up to? And how often have the words of just one other person kept a youngster from doing wrong? We may never know. In fact, most of us can easily look back upon our own childhood and recall the "angels in disguise" who took us aside or under wing; never hesitating to offer advice, support and, at times, lovingly admonish us to stay clear of those "occasions of sin?"

Personally speaking, I owe much to the angels who cared enough about my kids to encourage them, applaud them, and when needed, set them straight and get them back on the right road. In fact, I'm praying there are a lot more "disguised angels" around to help me raise the rest of this brood

But what of those children who have little in the way of faith and positive support? I recently read that four out of ten American children do not live in homes with their own fathers, and that more than half will experience being fatherless before they reach eighteen.

Who will their "father figure" be? As much as my children

need two parents, in addition to "angels" who will help guide them and protect them from those that would snatch their very souls, these youngsters need it more.

The world today is full of adults, some of whom actually undermine Christian values and fundamental beliefs. Still others maintain a non-judgmental approach telling youngsters little more than, "It's your life!" "Don't get caught." "I can't interfere." or "They're *all* doing it."

The Church in her mercy and wisdom offers a mantel of protection, not just to our children, but to all of us. As Christians we are called upon to be loving mentors to the young people in our lives, never wavering in our instruction to "do good and *avoid* evil."

As a parent I'm relying on those "angels in disguise" to help me guide my children correctly and keep them headed toward Heaven.

I realize my kids may not turn out perfect. But, they will know how we feel about sin and the need to watch out for the "occasions of sin." And so will any of their friends, no matter the age, who may naively walk through our back door and try to pass off something sinful with a wave of an arm and a "But Mrs. K. It's a new age!"

Over my dead body!

"Finally, draw your strength from the Lord and His mighty power. Put on the armor of God so that you may be able to stand firm against the tactics of the devil" (*Ephesians* 6:10-11).

Deviled Eggs

My John cooks as many as 90 to 120 at Eastertime!—
Our Bunny loves to hide them. Here's what I do with
some of them.

6 Hard cooked eggs
3 Tbsp Salad Dressing, vinegar or light cream
Vinegar
1/2 tsp Dry Mustard
1/2 tsp Salt
1/4 tsp Pepper
Pickle Relish for zest
Onion, finely chopped
Celery, finely chopped

Cut peeled eggs, lengthwise in half. Slip out yolks; mash with fork. Mix in minced onion and celery with seasonings and salad dressing. Fill whites with egg yolk mixture heaping it up lightly. Sprinkle with paprika. Chill and serve.

* Options: 1 tsp horseradish, shredded cheese, 2 Tbsp chopped parsley, 2 Tbsp chopped ripe chives or green onions.

CHAPTER 15

"Mom, That's 'Sooo' Old Fashioned!"

"Bear with one another; forgive whatever grievances you have against one another. Forgive as the Lord has forgiven you. Over all these virtues put on love, which binds the rest together and makes them perfect" (Colossians 3:13-14).

Every time I try to tell my kids what it was like when their Dad and I were young or, heaven forbid, suggest they try doing things the way we did, I am quickly reminded, "Mom, that's 'old fashioned'!" Believe me, as a mom of many I've heard this retort more than a few times.

I suppose they're hoping to jolt me out of the "Stone Age."

Some of our out-dated reasoning appears over the smallest things.

Take the notion of walking.

I've made more than a few mistakes on this one. For instance, one day Michael (12) asked, "Mom can I get a ride to Silver Point field?"

"Are you kidding? It's only four blocks," I replied. "You can walk four blocks. Walking is good for you. (first mistake) When I was your age, (second mistake) I walked that far to school *every day.* And we came home for lunch besides! (third mistake)"

And in that "not again" voice I was told, "Mom, this is a new age. That's old!"

Hmmm.

When I was young (oops! sorry) walking was our most reliable mode of transportation. Few folks had more than one car and many of the moms didn't drive. If you couldn't walk, bike, bus, or "hitch a ride" (car pool) with a friend, you didn't go. Period.

"Didn't go?" Another phrase almost extinct in these contemporary times!

Most kids today treat walking or any strenuous use of their legs as something to be reserved for important functions like sports and strolling the malls.

Yep. It's a new age, and I'm old fashioned.

The issue of television and movie choices seems a continual discussion, especially with adolescents who use every excuse from "that's all that's out there" to "I'm old enough to judge for myself."

Well, if its offensive and vulgar to me or on *my* TV set in *my castle* (I maintain that my home is my castle never mind outward appearances); no matter the age of the child, I have my own electronic chip called "Off"!

Nowhere is the difference more obvious than the area of boy/girl relations.

For instance, I saw the eyes roll and heard the suppressed chuckles the day I talked about dating with our three teen-aged daughters and said, "In *this* family, young ladies don't call boys on the phone unless it's homework or work-related."

The jaws dropped and in unison I was told, "MOM that's 'sooo' old fashioned!" Maybe so, but the rule stands.

"Young men like to do the calling and the pursuing!" I tell my doubting damsels who think some of my ideas and opinions are about as old and warped as the 45 records they found boxed in Grandma's attic.

"Gender-neutral era or not," I tell them, "I've already lived through three teenage sons and believe me, there's no quicker 'has been' than an aggressive girl who continuously calls, interrupting everything from early morning sleep to backyard 'hoops' with the guys, just to purr into the phone: *'Hi there! Whatcha doin'?'* "

The phone issue is nothing compared to the night we sat in stunned disbelief as a vehicle with a loud muffler pulled up to the curb, horn honking, radio blaring and our seventeen-year-old-daughter shouted "Bye Mom and Dad," as she flew out the door to her waiting date.

If that wasn't bad enough, when the evening came to an end, we heard the same distinct screeching to the curb, door slam, and car speed away, while our daughter stood alone fumbling for her keys at the front door.

It didn't happen again. From then on the *gentlemen* came to the door, introduced themselves to us, and delivered our daughters safely over the same threshold at the end of the evening.

No more Indy 500 raceway or "pit stop" dates.

Have you heard about boy/girl visits to bedrooms (for homework or *privacy*); hotel/motel prom nights; or co-ed camping trips (separate tents, of course)? So have we.

"Couples camping" for a weekend was naively sprung on us by one of our young adults who innocently asked if she could go.

"Where will you be living on Monday?" I asked this twenty-plus daughter who had given little thought to the real temptation involved or the scandal it could cause.

"It's a new age, Mom!" she explained. "The guys will be in one tent and the girls in another."

Over my bruised body!

"That may be, Honey, but that's still known as an 'occasion of sin' because it places you and your friends in great temptation. It also leads others who know you to believe that nice Catholic girls and boys are flaunting God's laws. That's called scandal.

"We have to care what others think because God wants us to be good examples and witnesses. It may sound old fashioned but you'll never be sorry for turning down such a tempting weekend."

Once explained, our daughter was more than accepting. She may have felt we were a bit outmoded, but she complied.

Thankfully, there is a whole group of other stodgy folks like us out there who continue to stand firm, directing their kids in everything from manners and safety to warning about the real occasions of sin, which always seem fashionable.

It must be terribly hard for young people today who live in an age that continuously separates prudence from "progress" and morality from "freedom." They need all the help and support we can offer including a few of our "archaic" virtues to guide them.

But let's be honest. What's so progressive about this age? An age filled with violence, racism, pornography, and the occult peddled on our streets and in every form of music and media.

With a culture that treats abortion as a "right" and children as problems to be spaced and limited, at the least resulting in over 1.3 million "little ones" legally destroyed each year, it's little wonder young people are confused.

Good parents never waver in their goal to get their children to Heaven. And with prayer and God's grace we will succeed!

In fact, offering counsel and advice, especially to our own vulnerable young, in particular to warn them of what we know may be dangerous, tempting, or sinful behavior, is not only our *right* but our *responsibility* and it will be no less than God Himself who will hold us accountable.

"Even a child is known by his doings, whether his work be pure, and whether it be right" (*Proverbs* 20:11).

Children, all children, may occasionally *test* a parent, bend a rule, and even "get in over their head" with serious trouble. Yet, the youngsters who are rooted in principles of faith and surrounded by love *will survive and thrive.*

"Correct your son, and he will bring you comfort; yea, and give delight to your soul" (*Proverbs* 29:17).

Most children, including teens and young adults, are really innocent. Whether it's good manners or serious moral questions, they want to be good and to know boundaries and limits.

The Holy Father Pope John Paul II says, "The future of humanity passes by way of the family." In fact, he deems it so vital, he wrote an entire letter *to* families:

"The Family is placed at the center of the great struggle

between good and evil, between life and death, between love and all that is opposed to love. To the family is entrusted the task of striving, first and foremost to unleash the forces of good, the source of which is found in Christ, the redeemer of man. Every family unit needs to make these forces their own so that . . . the family will be strong with the strength of God." (Familiaris Consortio, 86)

And when we are through with this parenting task, who knows? Perhaps someday our children will face their own young who will look at them with rolling eyes and suppressed giggles and try to convince them it's no longer the "Stone Age"!

And then they will know even more about real love!

"There is cause for rejoicing here. You may for a time have to suffer the distress of many trials; but this is so that your faith, which is more precious than the passing splendor of fire-tried gold, may by its genuineness lead to praise, glory, and honor when Jesus Christ appears" (1 *Peter* 1:6-7).

My Lasagna Recipe
It's a basic and nothing fancy

1 lb Italian Sausage
1/2 lb Ground Beef

1 Tbsp Whole Basil

1/2 tsp Salt
2 lg Cans of Tomatoes
2 6 oz Tomato Paste
Fennel Seed and Italian Spices

2-3 Celery Stalks, chopped
1-2 Onions, chopped

10 oz Lasagna Noodles
3 Cups Ricotta or Cottage Cheese
1/2 Cups Parmesan or Romano Cheese
2 Tbsp Parsley flakes
2 Beaten Eggs
1/2 tsp Pepper
1 lb Mozzarella cheese, thinly sliced

* Option: 1/2 pkg frozen spinach, green pepper, green onions, mushrooms

Brown meat slowly. Add onions, celery, green pepper, tomatoes and spices. Simmer 30 minutes, stirring occasionally.

Cook noodles in large amount of boiling water till tender. Drain and hang over sides of strainer so they don't stick together.

Combine remaining cheese, eggs, spinach & parsley. Put a little sauce on bottom of pan then begin layering: Noodles, cottage cheese filling, meat sauce, mozzarella cheese. Repeat layers, putting noodles in opposite pattern so it stays together better. Bake at 375° for 30 min. Let stand 5 to 10 min. Cut into squares and serve.

Tim & Tina chose this family favorite for their Groom's Dinner, which was held in our home. (We fed 60 people!)

* Feeling lazy? Use a commercial spaghetti sauce and cut out the spices and tomato ingredients.

CHAPTER 16

"Don't Let Suffering Go To Waste. Offer It Up."

"My brothers, count it pure joy when you are involved in every sort of trial. Realize that when your faith is tested this makes for endurance. Let endurance come to its perfection so that you may be fully mature and lacking in nothing" (*James* 1:2-4).

Funny how a bout with chicken pox or mumps can interfere with your life. I still remember the year when five of our kids came down with chicken pox. Not all at once. No. That would have been too easy. With our kids, the incubation and contamination period was staggered over weeks and by the time it was over I felt as if we'd been quarantined with a plague for an entire winter.

And then, there was the summer our boys played ball in a field full of poison oak. It showed up just as clearly, on our adopted Vietnamese black-skinned son, Charlie, who looked as if he was sprayed with buckshot as the calamine lotion peppered his arms, legs, and face! The sores and itching drove them crazy, and mom didn't take it in stride either, though she knew what to do about it.

"Offer it up!" as my mother would wisely instruct. "Just say, 'All for Thee O Sacred Heart of Jesus'!"

It's a practice that many adult Catholics grew up with, yet

I'm not sure our children will know the value of such a prayerful offering unless we tell them.

"God is never outdone in generosity." I now tell my own young whenever something doesn't go their way. "Offer this up as a prayer and just watch for the blessings." It's good for every kind of hurt or heartache. It can also be used to benefit another.

"You're letting God know you refuse to be frustrated or held hostage by trouble." I tell my kids. And at times the thought of offering up such things as the twenty-four-hour flu, rained out baseball games, traffic jams, fender benders, or bruised knees can even bring on a smile. My one regret is not remembering to do it more often.

It may not change the outcome, but it gives us back some control and is a way of actively relinquishing our every occurrence to God's care. This type of prayer causes a freedom. We are no longer enslaved to an unpleasant or painful experience, but rather, we've taken control and given it as a gift to God.

"I'll bet this is a prayer that really frustrates that 'ole devil'." I tell my young. "Just when he thinks he's got our goat!"

The late author and television personality Bishop Sheen, used to say, "I always feel sad when I drive by a hospital and see all the lights on, knowing the suffering that is going on there. And what a waste unless they're offering it up for the greater honor and glory of God!"

Bernice Syke wouldn't waste her time and she sure knows the meaning of suffering. This eighty-year-old grandmother is a member of our parish and when my teenage daughters, Angela and Kari, and I visited her in the hospital on one occasion, she was irritated as could be at the "routine" triple by-pass gone awry. The operation left her body consumed with infection and pain, yet, the brightness of her eyes told of her undaunted spirit.

"I can't believe the misery," she confessed. "If I had had any idea I would have refused this surgery."

"Are you offering it up?" I asked.

"You bet!" she quickly responded. "For my kids, my grandkids, and for my 'Bumpy' (her late husband). I want to go to Heaven and be with him." And in God's timing, which is always perfect, she will.

I have a friend who struggles daily with Parkinson's disease, not just the physical limitations but the mental anguish of *wanting* to be as active and in charge as she once was. But I know she is using her trial as a prayer for others because she told me so. Imagine how God listens to her, and the comfort she brings to those she prays for.

I know another woman who wants nothing more than to marry and have children. Yet, as the years go by, she quietly offers up her desires, realizing that God may have other plans.

My meager offerings pale by comparison. Dirty diapers, once my thorn, have been replaced by daily mounds of laundry, meal planning, (no sloughing off on this one) and what sometimes seems a monotony of cooking, cleaning, and catering.

But the *Catholic Catechism* reminds us in St. John Chrysostom's words, "It is possible to offer fervent prayer even while walking in public or strolling along, or seated in your shop, while buying or selling or even while cooking."

Some saints spent their entire lives perfecting the practice of praising God in *all* situations. St. Therese the Little Flower of Jesus called this practice her "little way" and wrote in her diary about "thanking Jesus for every interruption."

Interruptions! No wonder she is a saint homemakers can relate to. And her primary task as a cloistered nun was doing laundry, in a time long before automatic washers and dryers.

I can try to excuse myself for the busyness that prevents my using each act as a prayer. Yet when I do remember to "offer it up" not only my day but the tasks that make up the day go far better. In fact, my reminders to "praise God in all things," as St. Paul writes, often come from my own children. One day I overheard Angela (then 13) tell our six-year-old

Joseph who had burst in the door wailing from a bicycle fall. "Be brave, and offer it up!"

"Happy the man one who holds out to the end through trial. Once he has been proved, he will receive the crown of life the Lord has promised to those who love Him" (*James* 1:12).

CHAPTER 17

Sports: "No Time For Dinner Mom, I've Got A Game."

"My entire attention is on the finish line as I run toward the prize to which God calls me—life on high in Christ Jesus" (*Philippians* 3:14).

"How in the world can we have a dinner hour or 'family time' when our kids are so heavily involved in sports?" my friend, Mary, asked in frustration.

"I know sports are healthy, and teaches kids teamwork and good sportsmanship, but I feel as if it's taken on a priority and life all its own at our house. Are other families experiencing this tug?" she asked.

Mary's concern is shared by many Christian households, including this one.

My pastor, half kiddingly counseled; "If you want to keep your children out of trouble, keep 'em busy and keep 'em exhausted!"

This mom agrees. Most children seem to come "action packed," except where morning alarms and household chores are concerned. Boys especially seem to be bursting with hormones and endless amounts of energy during adolescent and teen years. Our trampled backyard lawn, worn-out swing set, and drooping basketball hoop are vivid reminders.

Yes, children need regular exercise and activity. In our case and unlike our ancestors, there is no family farm or heavy chores to help strengthen their muscles or fine-tune their coordination. Today, the majority of young people are like my kids, city bred with leisure to spare, in spite of assigned family chores. (You bet, my kids have daily "jobs." There'll be no "idle hands are the devil's tools" around here!) But it's not enough.

Both my husband, John, (who has generously volunteered hundreds of hours over the years to coach our children) and I are grateful for organized sports. It is more than healthy, and offers a unique opportunity to learn the value of teamwork, along with the thrill of striving for the prize, and the most important lesson of all, graciously accepting defeat. What better way to have fun and learn to play in unity with so many people of varied personalities, especially under tense situations. **Those are the positives.**

But as my friend Mary says, "**There are negatives**."

First, is the sacrifice made by the entire family. After all, when a youngster "signs up" for a sports team it means entrance fees, matching uniforms, scheduled practices, and games that almost always seem to occur around dinnertime.

Second, is the shift in family dynamics. When one of the members is not at the table, it's noticeable. "Michael's gone again? Now we're stuck doing *his* dishes!" as his sisters often lament.

More than picking up a brother's chores, it is the conversation and camaraderie; it is the intimacy and free exchange of ideas, opinions and current events of the day, that are lost.

Worse, when sports consume two to four dinner hours a week, as often happens in families like ours, family continuity suffers.

Over the years, our thirteen kids have suited up for football, baseball, soccer, basketball, volleyball, track, cross country, tennis and softball (not the same as baseball, so I've learned). I'm sure I'm leaving something out, but you get the picture.

Keep in mind, I know so little about some sports that my idea of football is to give both sides a ball so they won't fight over it.

Team sports has taught my children the importance of self-discipline, sacrifice, and has indeed been character building. It's also taught me the art of juggling.

Ask any sports mom. She's been there. It takes a master juggler to switch dinner hours, plan menus ("I gotta eat light, Mom, or I'll get a side ache") and be ready to drop the soup ladle at a moments notice to play taxi. ("Scott's mom will pick us up if you'll drive us there.")

And then there's the frustration of preparing a delicious meal only to see it *wolfed down* on the run or worse yet, put away for the next evening and served as "leftovers" because there was an unscheduled game! Some days I hate sports!

So much for "family time" or dinner "together."

My personal peeve are the evenings we do eat together and the talk automatically drifts to the "game" not just *theirs*, but the ones that capture headlines.

I'd hock my microwave and more if my children knew one-tenth as much about the lives of the saints as they do about the mega stars of the sports world. My kids know them by name and can recite by heart: the teams, the players, the scores, and the trivia that goes along with them. By age ten, our Michael's daily routine began by reading the Sports Section of the newspaper when most of us weren't even out of bed.

But why not? After all, sports has become America's greatest national pastime and it's players, with their *endorsements* of everything from shoes, jackets, animal causes, planet earth, and planet Hollywood, not to mention some unmentionable items, are broadcast daily over the airwaves and newspaper.

It takes a concerted effort for Christian parents to help their youngsters stay on course. *Heaven* that is, not golf. After all, our goal is not to groom them for the Olympics, but to get them to Heaven. A prize that lasts *forever*! We've established our own "Ground Rules" for sports involvement, in order to help maintain balance, family togetherness, and my own sanity. They are:

• **Set boundaries:** some children may be too young for the demands of organized teams, or to belong to more than one at the same time. Our goal is exercise, sportsmanship, and fun. Not to wear them out.

• **Our ultimate goal** is not to get them to the Olympics, but Heaven.

• **To "play ball" is a privilege.** If a child's conduct or grades are not as they should be, forfeiting practice or a game may result. Learning responsibility for their actions is more important than playing ball.

• **It's home plate at dinnertime unless sports or a part-time job prohibits.** Some kids routinely hang around a basketball court or field, even when they're not playing. If this takes the place of family or dinnertime, it must stop. Family first.

• **"Calling time" to talk and pray together**. If you *make time* each day for God, He will always be on your team. The old adage is true "The family that prays together, stays together." Statistics don't lie.

• **Don't feel guilty for not attending a child's game.** There is no *duty* to be there. Remember this is a "game" not the Olympics. Your child needs to know it's okay to play, to make mistakes, to fumble and to foul without worrying about winning your approval or what you will say on the ride home.

* Personally, I attend few games. In fact my rule of thumb is to attend one game, per child, per season. They know I'm interested but it is their activity. I don't need to watch them play to demonstrate my love. They know I'm their cheerleader on and off the field 24 hours a day.

• **Remember children's sports are for children. It's about their exercise, good sportsmanship, and fun.** Parents who nag, scold, lecture, or excessively drill their young take away the joy. And, such behavior can be discouraging and disheartening to an impressionable youngster. *"Fathers, provoke not your children to anger, lest they be discouraged"* (*Colossians* 3:21).

• **Christians should lead the way in sportsmanship on the field and in the stands.** Nothing is more scandalous than to see a team of youngsters, or worse yet, adults in the bleach-ers, who are cursing, shouting, swearing, or yelling at coaches or players. Remember, our children and others are watching. As followers of Christ, no matter the "unfair call" or shabby behavior of others, we are people of love and faith and should act accordingly. *"The tongue of the wise pours out knowledge, but the mouth of fools spurts forth folly. A soothing tongue is a tree of life, but a perverse one, crushes the spirit"* (*Proverbs* 15:2-4).

• **Make Sunday special.** This is the Lord's day. Do all in your power to preserve a dinnertime together. Sports should not dominate this day. Do something special with your family.

• **Don't let something else steal home base! Sports we can always play or watch, but family can only be enjoyed now.**

"So now, O children, listen to me; instruction and wisdom do not reject! Happy the man who obeys me, and happy those who keep my ways" (*Proverbs* 8:32-33).

Cinnamon Pull Aparts
Kuharski favorite for breakfast or brunch

2 frozen Bread dough loafs
1 Cup Vanilla ice cream
1 Cup Brown sugar
1/2 Cup Butter
Cinnamon and Sugar

Grease a round bundt pan. After letting frozen bread dough sit out 45 min. to an hour, cut it in half and then in half again. Cut into cubes, roll in cinnamon and sugar. Bring to a boil ice cream, brown sugar and butter. Pour over frozen bread dough. Cover with tin foil, let rise overnight in refrigerator. Bake for 30 minutes at 350°.

Options: Sprinkle chopped nuts in bottom of pan before adding dough pieces.

* This is one of those gooey treats that *everyone* loves!

CHAPTER 18

ATTENTION PARENTS: Do You Know What Your Child Is Watching?

"O God hear my prayer; hearken to the words of my mouth. For haughty men have risen up against me, and fierce men seek my life; they set not God before their eyes" (*Psalm 54:4-5*).

Jackie sat at our supper table perched on the picnic style bench between a row of our grade-schoolers, all chiming in at varied intervals about their favorite movie or TV sitcom. As I worked to keep their plates loaded, I was enjoying the spirited debate over "best all time" movies.

A frequent visitor, Jackie talked rapidly between mouthfuls. She relished the commotion of our large household, yet she was wise to the fact that any lengthy pause or monologue could forfeit her chance for seconds.

The children were extolling the likes of everything from vintage Disney to classic musicals, such as "Meet Me in St. Louis," "Bye Bye Birdie," "The Unsinkable Molly Brown," "The Music Man," "The Wizard of Oz," "The Sound of Music," and a host of others. Included in the list was our family's most recent "find" black and white reprints of Andy Hardy and the Ma and Pa Kettle series (my six-year-old's favorites!).

Table talk excitement came to an abrupt and nervous halt,

however, when Jackie began to rattle off some of the more current movie titles that we knew to be unacceptable for their R-
rated violence or permissive sex scenes.

"You don't mean you've seen those films?" I naively asked.
Knowing her family as active church members, I said to this
cherub like 7th grader, "I'm sure your Mom wouldn't let you
see movies like that."

"Oh yes she does," Jackie unhesitatingly replied. "She rents
them for us and sometime she and my Dad watch 'em with us."

My own children began to fidget in their places. (Probably
fearing I would call her mother and start World War III.)

I didn't. "What's the point," I told myself. Jackie's mom is
now just another permissive parent. And what a disappointment! These parents, people of faith, are the very people we
look to for support. Especially if we hope to stop the flow, or
at minimum stem the tide of sexually graphic, violent, and
godless material that preys on our young and innocent.

While I may be surprised and disappointed at "who" is
doing the permitting, in this circumstance, I have long since
lost my shock at the number of moms and dads who abandon
their roles as moral guardians on flimsy excuses such as, "It's
a new age" or "What can you do when that's all that's out
there?"

"Frankly, we don't like it," one mother told me when I
called to object to my elementary aged youngster viewing a
PG-13 movie at her daughter's birthday party, "But the kids
today are so much more knowledgeable. And what else is
there?"

One father brushed off a concern I expressed over the new
teen magazines and the sexually explicit content, by respond-
ing, "Oh . . . They see and experience more just riding the bus
home from school every day!" If that were true, I'd be driving
a bus.

Some parents either fear the risk of being unpopular with
their own child, are more interested in keeping them "up with
the times," or have a frighteningly ignorant misconception that
"my kids can handle it!" Little wonder kids are confused.

We hear the same argument from parents who condone or worse yet sponsor underage beer bashes at graduations and motel prom nights. At a conference on "Building Healthy Family Relationships" sponsored by Catholic Charities, one presenter, Misti Snow, a Minneapolis *Star-Tribune* editor of the "Mindworks" column, spoke of the fears, concerns, and loss of hope she sees more routinely in the many essay submissions of elementary to high school aged children.

"I've seen many changes in the twelve years I have done the "Mindworks" column. I am reading more essays from kids, little kids, who are addicted to violence—gruesome, horrible acts of violence. I never read about kids having nightmares before, but more and more are confiding nightmare experiences."

The editor went on to say that many kids reported they were too afraid or had "no one to tell" for fear of being called a sissy. "They can't tell their parents because oftentimes it is the parents who allow them to watch it, the parents who bring the videos home, or the parents who watch it with them."

Snow warned of children becoming "desensitized to death and the most horrendous forms of brutality" and challenged listeners to consider the impact of the reading, listening, and video material allowed in the home. To be effective, this challenge must include parents, grandparents, neighbors and friends.

Perhaps the harshest criticism of the present age of permissive parents will come, not from their peers, but from their own children who looked for moral guidance, rules, and restraints, and were told instead to "choose for yourself," and "you be the judge."

How can we make a difference?

• **Do what is morally right.** As parents we are responsible for items to which our children are exposed. Be a role model and act with authority. God will give you the grace. Your child is depending on you.

• **Choose good and reject the mediocre *and* evil.** Now is the time to rid your household of *any* reading or viewing material you know to be vulgar, offensive, or morally confusing to a child.

• **Bring into your home** *only* **things you know to be interesting, educational, and entertaining.** Leave magazines and books around where your child may be enticed to pick them up and browse through. Make sure there is plenty with sound Christian content and don't forget the positive and humorous. Children are exposed to enough that is depressing.

• **The TV and remote belong to you.** You hold the power! Get your children accustomed to **asking permission** before watching TV or selected videos. These are wonderful forms of entertainment and relaxation, not to be abused or over-used. At our house, we made the investment in a VCR and now rent or buy movies. Some video centers regularly host sales and have a good selection of wholesome family entertainment to rent or buy. In our case, belonging to a movie club and purchasing films at a discount was well worth the price and it ended the arguments "there's nothing to watch."

• **Your home is your castle.** What you have on display or allow to be viewed represents you. "Would God be pleased?" is a good guide in judging what material is allowed in the home. This includes photos and posters on walls. "I own the house *and* the wall," I remind my young. "It represents Dad and I *as well as you.* In the end, we are responsible." Even in the case of adults living at home, if something is offensive to you, it must go. You have automatic "veto power" and are the one who will have to answer later for what *you* permitted.

• **Don't let teens or young adults bully you.** Gently but firmly remind them that until they are in their own home, they have no right to air a program you consider objectionable.

• **Don't allow TV sets in children's bedrooms (even young adults).** It causes isolation and can promote unlimited or unhealthy viewing habits. Love that teen who can afford to buy his or her own TV enough to say "No." Far more important for a healthy mind and body is a workout at the backyard basketball hoop, playing tennis, walking or biking.

• **Don't be a wimp or offer flimsy excuses.** Kids can sniff

out a waffling parent a mile away. They are far more comfortable with a strong and consistent stand, than with rule
bending and game-playing concocted in order to keep peace.

• **Be consistent.** Don't confuse a child with changed minds
or plea bargaining. Children much prefer knowing their limits
and what's allowed and what isn't. They also want to know the
same rule applies to you.

• **You set the tone.** Viewing mediocre material, or worse yet
graphically sexual and explicit, invades a youngster's imagi-
nation and may confuse or forever compromise his or her
thinking. When this occurs with the knowledge, permission, or
the presence of an indifferent or approving parent, the images
elicit an approval or consent to the child. "This must not be
bad because they let me see it."

• **Be fair.** Tell your young beforehand and then stick to your
rules. It not only avoids problems, but also the embarrassment
of being disciplined or scolded in front of others.

• **Don't give in or give up.** If setting media standards is new
at your house, be patient, yet firm. Let your children know you
felt the need to establish media ground rules after seeing the
gradual "take over" that is encroaching on your family's precious, and often scarce, free time.

• **Remember: Your child is watching you!** Far more than
any movie or TV sitcom, your child is learning by osmosis and
his or her teacher is you. How you live, treat others, worship
God, and what forms of entertainment you choose, will most
likely be the ones chosen by your child. Children will only
understand the meaning and practice of personal discipline and
self-restraint if they see their parents and adult mentors, teachers, aunts and uncles, neighbors and friends doing the same.

**This discipline certainly includes showing prudence in
our eating, drinking, entertainment, and appetite for luxu-
ries.** Like it or not, we are their greatest role models. Jack
Quesnell, a Minneapolis marriage and family counselor and
author of six books including his most recent, *Beyond Your
Wedding Day*, tells parents that in the long run, we do our children a disservice "when we give in to their desires and demands

even if it promises to keep peace and prevent a standoff."

"Unless," he says, "we offer a healthy mixture of love and discipline to the adults of tomorrow (our kids) they are doomed to become the most intolerant, self-centered, demanding, and self-directed generation of Americans to live." A legacy of unhappiness for themselves and others.

As Christian parents, we are challenged today perhaps as never before. Let's love our children enough to discipline, to set guidelines, and to remember that our responsibility does not end in front of a movie or TV screen even if it is "a new age!"

"More precious than gold is health and well-being, contentment of spirit than coral. No treasure greater than a healthy body; no happiness, than a joyful heart!" (*Sirach* 30:15-16).

Swedish Pancakes
Kuharski kids' favorite

2 Eggs
1 Cup Milk
3/4–1 Cup Flour
1+ Tbsp Sugar
1/2 tsp Salt
2 Tbsp Butter—melted and added last to mixture

Mix together all ingredients, then add melted butter and mix thoroughly. This recipe has been passed down from a wonderful Swedish lady. It may need to be doubled or tripled (as it is at our house) depending upon the crew.

These pancakes are thin, light and sweet.
(Our entire family loves these Sunday morning favorites. Hope yours do!)

CHAPTER 19

Pass The Manners—Please

"Train up a child in the way he should go; and when he is old he will not depart from it" (*Proverbs* 22:6).

Is nothing sacred? Ever since our family sat behind two teenage boys in church who smugly wore their baseball style caps throughout the entire Christmas Eve Mass, I've wondered.

Maybe what got the best of me was not so much the ill-mannered young men and their two girlfriends who chatted and giggled all the way through the Consecration or the fact that this was a sacred and beautiful service, but rather the sight of their parents sitting with them who acted as if their behavior was perfectly normal.

Will there be more of the same at Easter or regular Sunday services? Whatever became of reverence? And what's happened to parents?

Yes, I know the old argument about "just be glad they're there." I also know that a child's notion of God, Church, and how little or much faith means, is readily portrayed by a parents' attitude. If clothes or conduct mean little, could God and faith mean much more?

While on vacation in Mexico, my husband and I enjoyed attending daily Mass. Huge signs were posted at the entrance of the church, both in Spanish and English, asking those who entered NOT to wear shorts or swimsuits and to be "properly attired" before entering. Every day we saw people, tourists, actually walk *around* the sign and go right in, with their scanty shorts and bare midriff tops as if to say, "this couldn't possibly mean me. After all, I'm on vacation!"

Whatever became of *reverence?*

And what has become of manners?

Speaking of manners, I remember when a gentleman would give up his seat or place in line for a woman or someone elderly? Once in a while you can still spot such a daredevil who throws fate to the wind and offers his place to a senior or lady. But for the most part, the men of today have been seared by the threat of a radical feminist reprisal that would instantly humiliate them for any such act of courtesy or chivalry. What a shame.

In 1996, a school board decision to expel unruly, disruptive, and threatening students, was vigorously fought by the parents, who demanded the youngsters "right of expression and individuality." Whatever happened to respect for authority and whatever became of parents?

Today we are surrounded by people "doing their own thing," including celebrities who seem to thrive on outdoing one another in tasteless, indecent or offensive behavior. It's trendy. And so we witness an array of slovenly, if not downright immodest dress and listen to speech which has become "show-off" vulgar with four letter words or the kind of gutter gossip that would shock a drunken pirate. At the beach, in the media, and on the streets it's *everywhere!*

Worse yet, we're just as likely to hear it from women as men. So much for the "ladies." Little wonder children are confused.

"It's frustrating," my friend, Pat, confided. "The world is going one way, and we're trying to point our kids in another."

What's a parent to do? *"Correct your son, and he will bring you comfort, and give delight to your soul"* (*Proverbs* 29:17).

Easier said than done. Yet, speaking personally, when children are trained from infancy in good manners and self-discipline, the chance of tantrums or rebellion are minor and usually controllable.

All children, even opinionated and balking teens truly do want to do what's right and to win the respect of those they admire. In fact, we fail them miserably when we let them "decide what's right for you."

Pope John Paul II, in his recent encyclical, *The Gospel of Life* (Evangelium Vitae) urges us to create a "culture of love." He declared that parents have the right and responsibility to instill proper attitudes regarding issues of chastity and morality in their young.

So what has this got to do with reverence in church and manners? Everything. Clearly, if we expect our kids to be disciplined against the big temptations in life: promiscuity, open defiance, rebellion and unlawfulness, we must help them to be steadfast in the small.

After all, if the house of God deserves no special dress and good behavior, who and what does? And if giggling and flirting during Mass is okay, what more profound occasion than the miracle of Christ's *real presence,* deserves our reverence?

Yes, my kids roll their eyes and occasionally sneak each other one of those "Here-we-go-again" looks if I begin a sentence with, "You're a Kuharski, mind your manners. People notice good behavior. . . ."

Isn't that what mothers are for?

One thing is certain; kindness and courtesy are contagious. So too are reverence and respect. There's something in experiencing it that makes us want more.

Some parents seem absolutely floored when their child begins to live a promiscuous lifestyle, rejecting God and often family in the process. "We don't know what happened to him."

Yet, other observers may have seen the telltale signs of a foundation crumbling early on, as the growing child *got by* with defiance and little acts of rebellion, which only gave way later to a more flagrant rejection of what is right and good.

Sin first becomes tolerated, then habit forming, and eventually comfortable. For example, when dirty jokes or vulgar language are excused, there is little surprise when chastity and modesty are eventually abandoned.

The children are the losers—along with society.

Ask any parent who has ever complimented a youngster for good behavior and they'll tell how the child strives to do it again and again.

"Being Christian," I tell my children, "means we live a little differently than others. People should recognize us by the way we behave. After all, Jesus tells us that the second greatest Commandment after first loving God, is to love our neighbor as ourselves. And we begin by showing courtesy and a basic respect for others."

Parents, it's up to us to promote good manners. And, what more important place to begin than in God's House?

Here are some basic guides we try to regarding manners in our household:

• **Watch yourself.** People know you and will judge you by your actions, words, and deeds. Do you like what they see? Is this how God calls you to live?

• **Watch your language.** Can you say the same thing in front of your mother or grandmother? If not, don't say it. Remember, once spoken, words can't be taken back.

• **Watch your dress.** God calls us to "let our light shine" for others. We can still have fun in what we choose to wear, and do, as long as modesty and decency are never sacrificed.

• **Watch your behavior.** There is no room for illicit drink or drugs, immoral behavior, or vulgar jokes if you want others to know you as a person of dignity and integrity.

• **Watch your manners.** It says more about you than anything. Saying "Thank you," "Please," "May I help," writing a note of gratitude for a gift or kindness, and simple acts of courtesy, especially toward adults and the elderly, are *never* out of date. How do you want others to remember you?

• **Cleanliness is next to Godliness.** If you or your room is dirty, or offensive in appearance the message you present to those around you is "I don't care enough about you to dress up or clean up." What we have and what we wear are gifts from a generous God; how we take care of it tells others what we think of Him and them.

- **No hats at dinner tables and *never* in church (guys).**
- **Choose your friends carefully.** "Tell me who you go with and I'll tell you who you are" an adage of old, still true today. If your friends are known for their honesty, decency, integrity and Christian behavior, so too will you. The reverse is also true, if those you hang around with have shady reputations, yours will be tarnished too.
- **Create a climate of love.** Courtesy, kindness, and treating even those you do not like with respect lets others know you are a person of character. It takes discipline and sometimes real courage, to stand out in the crowd and do the polite, charitable, or right deed. Pray and God will give you the grace.
- **Take your Guardian Angel along.** If the thought of bringing your Angel with you seems out of place, don't go. Some people and places are nothing short of "occasions of sin" and should be avoided. Before going out, ask your Guardian Angel and the Blessed Mother to help and protect you. They will. When we do this, decency and manners will simply be a part of who we are.

"Therefore, take these words of mine into your heart and soul. Bind them at your wrist as a sign, and let them be a pendant on your forehead. Teach them to your children, speaking of them at home and abroad, whether you are busy or at rest" (*Deuteronomy* 11:18-19).

Wild Rice Soup
Featuring Minnesota's own wild rice, this
makes a special entrée for any dinner.

2 Cup Uncooked Wild Rice
2 Cups Water
2 Tbsp Butter
1 medium Onion, diced
1 quart Milk
2 cans Cream of Potato Soup
1 Cup chopped Celery
1 Cup chopped Carrots
Fresh Mushrooms
Green Pepper, small diced bit (optional)
1 lb Velveeta Cheese
10 strips of crisp Bacon—crumbled over top (optional)

Prepare wild rice according to basic package directions.
Sauté onion in butter till tender. Add celery, carrots, gr pepper.
Add water, milk and potato soup. When mixture is hot, add
cheese in chunks to speed melting. When creamy, add cooked
wild rice. * To make thicker, add more wild rice. Garnish with
bacon crumbled. Serves 6-8.

* Of course, a few of our "picky" ones stay away from this
because they either don't like the mushrooms, don't like the
wild rice, don't like the cheese, don't like the onions, don't like
the carrots . . . You get the picture!

CHAPTER 20

Children: Love 'Em Enough To Discipline

"I will instruct you and show you the way you should walk; I will counsel you, keeping my eye on you (Psalm 32:8).

Upon hearing that I was the mother of a large family, a bachelor leaned over and confided at a recent dinner party, "You know I am a Christian and was the oldest in a family of eleven myself. . . . But, I must confess, I'd rather do just about *anything* than be around unruly or undisciplined children."

I'm with him!

"What makes me feel so bad," he continued, "is that some of the children that drive me nuts, are family or the children of close friends. I see so little discipline and so much permissiveness for what I would call downright obnoxious or bad behavior."

He's right, and *Proverbs* 29:17 tells us; *"Correct thy son, and he shall give thee rest; yea, he shall give delight unto thy soul."*

Yet, his impression can have little effect unless mothers and fathers themselves take God's vocational call to parenthood seriously and love their children enough to discipline them.

Many parents of children now grown would add their own "Amen" to such words!

My own consolation has always been in knowing we aren't in this alone. God promises to give parents the grace necessary to raise their children to be loved and lovable. And isn't that our goal?

Through our own "trials" and a few errors, my husband and I have established a few ground rules on discipline:

• **Be consistent.** Nothing mixes a youngster up faster than parents who say one thing and then change the rules. Say what you mean and mean what you say. Kids are far more grateful for clear, concise, and consistent standards than nagging, empty threats, or whimpish warnings like "O.K. . . . one more chance this time. . . ."

• **Stick together.** Parenting especially involving a testing or rebellious child, is ten times more difficult if parents are at odds. A youngster learns quickly if he or she can pit one parent against the other and drive a wedge between father and mother. Each time a child is successful in this all parties lose. The child becomes manipulative and disrespectful of authority. And the parents begin to build resentment and animosity toward each other no longer focusing on the child and his or her shortcomings, but upon their mate instead.

• **Love your children enough to discipline them.** Discipline is love. It's much harder to take the time and energy needed to train a child properly, than to let it go. A spanking, grounding, "time-out," taking the car keys, or "whatever is fair" may be the most loving thing for a disobedient child. It also serves as a crucial reminder that our rules and regulations are not meant to hurt but rather to protect them from harm (be it physical, emotional, or spiritual).

One of our sons, a ninth grader at the time, was going through a typical teen "I'm-old-enough. Why-can't-I-do-what-I-want?" period. On one occasion, as I was explaining the reason behind our latest "No," I looked up in time to catch sight of his teeth-clenching, eyes-blazing, defiance. I stopped what I was unsuccessfully trying to say and simply said, "I know it's hard for you to understand why, but you know that we are motivated by love and nothing more. We would never intentionally hurt you or want you to be miserable. We love you and we're only doing what we think is best for you."

At that point, he looked up. His eyes softened and his body became limp, as he quietly nodded, "I know you love me,

Mom." End of confrontation. He still wanted his way but the arguing and hostility were gone. To a rebellious child, reminders of love are extremely important.

• **Add TLC.** All children have a need for love, including a sense of closeness and touching. When kids enter their teen years, there may be a tendency to forget or forego this. With boys especially, it is sometimes sadly assumed, "he's getting too old for that now."

On the contrary, we all need affection; and teenagers are no different. In fact, there may be times when they need a gentle hug or sense of feeling loved even more. If it doesn't happen at home, they may go out in search of it elsewhere. Touch, hugs, tender pats and kisses are important and not to be forgotten. It lessens the tension and is a reminder of a parent's love.

• **Don't delay or postpone punishment.** If a child, no matter, the age, has done something to merit parental discipline, the punishment should be swift, merciful, and, after the youngster's apology and promise to be good, forgotten. Neither mother or father should bully a youngster by postponing the punishment with a "Just wait until your father gets home," or waiting for a future date which is too difficult for the child to connect to the offense.

Pre-schoolers *usually* comprehend a swift swat on the bottom far better than being denied something an hour or two later. Never use an object, however, a hand is stern enough. On the other hand, spanking is usually ineffective on a school age youngster and could be a source of humiliation to an older child unequal to the wrongdoing. Enforcing "time out" penalties, or grounding (not being permitted to leave his room, or the family property) works on most youngsters (except the very young) and is far more beneficial. This technique may give a child just the "break" needed to re-thinkhis or her behavior and the time needed to decide to make the desired change. It gives mom and dad a cooling off period too.

• **Praise and punishment go hand in hand.** When a youngster—especially one who knows better and yet "chooses" to do wrong—is in trouble, it should be seen by parents for what it is—a cry for help. They want to be noticed, loved, and respected. This is as true of three-year-olds demonstrating jealousy over a new baby, as it is of teenagers trying to "make a statement."

Discipline when done lovingly answers that need. On the other hand, we don't want to set up a situation where a child remembers that the negative attention receives a stronger reaction than one that is positive. If that's the case, he or she will head for more of the same.

• **Compliment and reward good behavior.** Children strive very hard to please their parents and other authority figures they respect. A simple acknowledgment, such as "You're being so good today!" and a hug goes a long way.

Some occasions may merit something more: a trip for ice cream, lunch out together alone, a trip to the movies. Be careful not to lavish or over-indulge. It is confusing and can be detrimental. Use your better judgment, you know the difference!

• **Keep 'em busy.** For the kids exhibiting unruly or bad behavior give them something to do. "I see energy to burn and not enough to do," I tell my young. "So grab a bucket and vacuum and we'll make a list of some of the things you can help with around here." The setting up of additional chores does three things:

1. It keeps a child busy. The old adage "idle hands are the devil's tools" is certainly true.

2. The work helps him burn off some of that energy and frustration.

3. It gives the parent something to thank and praise the kid for. Thus, the child is reminded that not everything he or she does is bad, that he or she *can* do good things, and is appreciated when he or she does.

• **Everyone needs to feel valuable—give 'em a job.** Even small children want to feel an active part of the family. If everything is done for them, they feel more like a guest than family. No child should grow up without specific chores to do every day. Even small tasks, help begin the formation of a good work ethic. While giving a child an allowance may have its place (we never got into that—our kids had paper routes and babysitting jobs to obtain spending money), no child should be paid for every little effort made. Everyone should contribute toward making their home and surroundings clean and comfortable. This reinforces a sense of belonging and importance. "I am needed."

• **Pick your battles.** All teens need to do something a little off the wall or outrageous. Better now while they are young, than as an overly protected adult lashing back in a way that may ruin a marriage or the lives of others.

While some parental rules and requests cannot waiver, others can be bent with little harm. In our book that includes issues of hair and clothing. Our son, Tony, once walked in sporting a pony-tail. I thought my husband would faint! It only lasted a month but Tony enjoyed saying he was "making his statement," and expressing his taste.

Mary Elizabeth, our impetuous highschooler maintains honor roll status and has never given us a problem. But, she loves to experiment with hair color, never however, outrageous or radical in appearance. We huff and puff a bit over some of the hairdos and outfits, but in general we see it as harmless expressions of independence.

Allowing a bit of leeway regarding hair, clothing, and depending on the event curfews, can go a long way in a young person's mind; and is far more healthy an outlet than immoral or illegal behavior.

• **Admit your error. Apologize when you are wrong.** Hopefully only God is keeping track of the number of times we fly off the handle, over-react, or judge too harshly. I have learned on just such occasions, to admit my error and apologize to my child. And what a wonderful outcome results. Perhaps it is times such as these that our children learn even more from parents about humility, compassion, forgiveness and remorse.

• **Honor thy father and mother.** As long as children, adult or otherwise, live at home, they must be respectful and reverent of your authority and rules including religious practices. Our kids go to church with us on Sunday, unless part-time work or a special occasion prevent it. And even then, we expect them to attend another Mass that is not in conflict with their work schedule.

• **Pray.** Being a parent has a way of intensifying a prayer life. And well it should. This is no small job! Let us never forget that these are God's children and He loves them a great deal more than we do. He also promises the grace necessary to help us do our parenting job well. All we need do is ask!

Not only should we pray daily for our children. We should pray *with* them.

This is the most powerful teaching tool parents have.

For those stubborn problems a suggested prayer is: "Lord, help me see this child through your eyes and not mine" is a prayer I say when I feel a particular frustration toward one of my children. It never fails to lessen the tension and help to restore the tenderness and balance needed. Prayer never fails!

Truly God gives the grace and all the means necessary to raise our children to be loved and lovable. And if we truly want what's best for them, we'll love them enough to discipline them. We have only to look around, as the young bachelor reminds us, to see the results of those who could use a little more loving discipline in their lives.

"He who spoils his son will have wounds to bandage, and will quake inwardly at every outcry. A colt untamed turns out stubborn, a son left to himself grows up unruly. Pamper your child and he will be a terror for you, indulge him and he will bring you grief" (Sirach 30:7-9).

Peanut Butter Bars
(Kuharski kids all-time favorite
and great to pack for outings)

1 (14 oz) Can Sweetened Condensed Milk
1/2 Cup Peanut Butter
1 Cup Flour
2 Cup Oatmeal
1 Cup Brown Sugar
1/2 tsp Baking Soda
1/2 tsp Salt
3/4 Cup Butter—softened
1 Cup Chocolate Chips (12 oz)

Grease 9 X 13 pan. Combine milk and peanut butter. Mix till blended. Set aside. In large bowl, combine flour, oatmeal, brown sugar, soda, salt, and butter and mix until crumbly. Press half of crumb mixture into pan. Pour peanut butter and mixture over crumbs in rows. The mixture will spread out to cover evenly. Sprinkle with chocolate pieces. Top with remaining crumbs. Pat down slightly. Bake at 325°—350° for 25 min. till golden brown. Cool and cut into bars.

* Note: The only thing wrong with this recipe is that it is never around long enough!

CHAPTER 21

Talking To Our Children About Puberty

"My little ones, I am writing this to keep you from sin. But if anyone should sin, we have, in the presence of the Father, Jesus Christ, an intercessor who is just" (1 John 2:1).

Classroom instructors and social programs are telling children about the "facts of life" at younger and younger ages. Sad to say, instead of objecting to this intrusion of the parental role, some parents are relieved.

"They've got all those years of education, and all the expertise. They can handle it so much better," say some. Not true.

We must remember that **no matter how accurate the technique or beautifully it is presented, even when done with a religious view, it is not as meaningful as when it comes from you the parent.**

Studies continue to show: **children overwhelmingly prefer learning about the facts of life from their parents.** Parents, in fact, rank head and shoulders above teachers, peers, school counselors or other authority figures. A study by the Search Institute, a nationally recognized secular group doing research on child development, revealed, "Parents still make the greatest impression and have the greatest influence."

Remember too, as parents, we are responsible—and no one else—for the transmission of faith and morals to our young.

In the meantime, if you want to know how the facts of life are being presented to your child in the classroom, don't be shy about asking. Most teachers are only too happy to provide this information. Some parents use this as a "jump start" to sit down and talk to their youngster.

More than discovering what is being taught, we can rely on our own parental skill fueled by God's grace when talking to our children about the changes that will take place in their own bodies as they pass from childhood through adolescence, and into adulthood.

We may not say it perfectly. We may fumble and feel awkward. That's all right. The main thing is to find a comfortable, unrushed, relaxed time when you can be alone with your child. Once you get started the words will flow.

Facts about Puberty:

Girls: Along with menstruation; the development of the breasts and body; the growing of hair on the legs, pubic region, and underarms are the most noticeable changes. There is an emotional growth that also occurs.

The young girl becomes more sensitive: self-conscious about her dress and appearance. She becomes interested in the opposite sex and may work diligently to attract their attention. She is also more prone to mood swings.

At the same time, the young girl will now begin to develop a more nurturing, "motherly" attitude toward younger children. Babysitting jobs, caring for a baby sister or brother, are fun and very positive ways to support that maternal inclination.

Boys: Hair, voice, and physical strength are the most noticeable changes that occur when a young boy enters puberty. Hair on the legs, arms, pubic region and face appears. A boy's shoulders broaden, his voice deepens, and he begins to see himself in a more manly way.

The developing boy may, for the first time, see himself as he does his father, capable of doing heavy jobs (never mind his unemptied trash or disheveled room—what glory is there in cleaning that?). He may volunteer to do "big" jobs, or swell with pride when called upon for such tasks.

Most importantly, he should be encouraged to see himself in a protective role, i.e., the "big brother." Sensing his own strength and manliness, he is now in a unique position to offer protection and care for younger members of his family or neighborhood.

While his body changes may tempt a sexual curiosity or experimentation; he is also very idealistic and capable of great acts of self-denial and sacrifice. Even in today's sex-saturated climate, a young man can resist temptation, especially when kept busy with school, work, and some type of outdoor or sports activity. Now is the time to let him know you depend on him "to do the right thing." The key is having parents and a good father figure who believe in him and offer support.

Let your youngsters know, too, that their **language, behavior**, and **dress** also sends important messages to others. Thus, a young lady always dresses modestly, (there is no such thing as a "modest" bikini!) never uses foul or suggestive language, and her behavior must never scandalize others or cause them to question her moral integrity.

So too, parents are obliged to remind their sons that a *real* man treats all women with respect. A boy's language; interests, including reading and video material; and behavior should always reflect respect for God's laws. Illegal drugs or drinking and any form of sexual experimentation with themselves or others—including intimate petting, genital touching, or arousal—is behavior unbecoming a gentleman.

More than that, both boys and girls need to know such behavior is serious and sinful because it violates God's laws and is an abuse of our bodies which are *always* to be treated as temples of the Holy Spirit.

Sad to say, there are those in today's world who do not see the act of masturbation as sinful. In fact, some have sent confusing and misleading messages actually advocating it *in place of* intercourse before marriage.

As Christian parents, we are *obliged* to let our young know that masturbation is wrong and an abuse of our bodies. It is selfish, sinful, and quickly becomes habit forming. It may also present a serious obstacle to enjoying good married sex later in life with a spouse, because of the individual's preoccupation with self.

Let your young know **"you will be tempted but God promises to give us all the grace we need to stay away from sin and resist temptation if we pray to Him."**

It's also good to give some hints, **"Keep yourself active and busy. Stay away from things (books, videos, movies, or individuals) you know will tempt you."**

And always, God offers us forgiveness and renewed strength when we fail. We need only ask.

Christ calls us to be *"in the world but not of it."* We want our young to know that we are Christians and because we are people of faith we are called by God to live differently than others. Your teens can be a living witness for those who have no such faith or standards. Tell them, **"You can be a positive influence and real friend to the kids who might have no one else in their life to turn to or look up to."**

"Beloved, you are strangers and in exile, hence I urge you not to indulge your carnal desires. By their nature they wage war on the soul. Though the pagans may slander you as troublemakers, conduct yourselves blamelessly among them. By observing your good works they may give glory to God. . ."
(*1 Peter* 2:11-12).

In The Early Years

The following suggested conversation between parent and child is offered as a guide to those with children of pre-puberty age:

Mom: I understand that you will be learning some very important things this year at school about life and how your body develops.

Julie: How did you know that?

Mom: I asked your teacher because I wanted the chance to talk to you about it first so that if you had any questions we could talk it over.

Julie: What's it about?

Mom: It's about how little girls grow up to become young ladies and boys grow to become young men.

Julie: When does that happen?

Mom: It starts for every person at a different time. Usually for boys and girls, it begins somewhere between the ages of 11 and 16. You've probably noticed your sisters and brothers or kids at school, who are going through this change. It's called puberty. A simple word that really means to "develop." When it begins, their skin becomes a bit oily and they tend to break out on the face with pimples or blackheads. They need to keep clean, washing often and taking a bath or shower daily. Bathing not only prevents body odor but washing your face several times a day helps prevent dirt and oil from getting into the pores of your skin and causing pimples.

Julie: It's called "zits" Mom!

Mom: I thought you'd know.

Julie: Is puberty the time when boys voices change?

Mom: That's right. Another change is more hair; for the boys hair will begin to grow on their face. Their legs will become more hairy and hair will also grow in their underarm and pubic area, where the penis and testicle sac is located.

Julie: What happens to the girl?

Mom: Well, for the girls, the oily skin occurs, but normally the only hair growth that takes place is on the legs, underarms, and the pubic area. Her breasts are now changing and beginning to enlarge. This is nature's way of preparing for the day when, and if, she becomes a mommy, she can nurse her baby.

Julie: That's a lot of changes.

Mom: One more thing begins to happen to young girls during this time and it is called "menstruation."

Julie: What does that mean?

Mom: Menstruation is a process that happens only to girls because only women can get pregnant and have babies. You see, Julie, God designed a very special place for babies before birth. He loves little children so much He wanted each one to feel the warmth and security of a mommy from the very beginning. So, inside every woman is a place called the womb which is a tiny sac that holds the baby until it is ready to be born. The womb prepares each month to receive a baby by filling up with all sorts of nutrition. But if there is no baby to nourish and feed, it gets rid of the old nutrition about every 28 to 30 days, and begins the storing up process all over again. This monthly discharge is often referred to as a girl's cycle or "period."

Julie: Oh, I've heard of that. So a period is the same as menstruation.

Mom: Yes. It simply means monthly discharge. It has a red bloody appearance and really is nature's way of getting rid of the excess nutrition or waste that the womb did not need. This usually begins somewhere between the age of 11 to 16.

Julie: Does it hurt?

Mom: A woman may feel a bit tired or crampy, but most are able to do the same daily routines of work and play they always do.

Julie: How does menstruation stop and how does the baby get into the womb?

Mom: It stops just like it starts. By itself. A period lasts about three to five days. During that time the woman wears disposable pads to catch the discharge that comes out. You've probably seen the packages under the bathroom counter.

Julie: So that's what that is.

Mom: As far as how the baby gets into the womb, well God planned that sometimes when mommies and daddies are alone and get very close, a seed will pass from the dad to the mom. If the seed joins the egg she has inside her, a new human life is created. This is called "conception" and it simply means that a tiny baby, an embryo, is alive and growing inside the mother's womb. When that happens she stops menstruating because the baby now needs all that nutrition the womb was storing up.

Julie: Wow!

Mom: That's a lot to think about isn't it?

Julie: Yeah.

Mom: The main thing you want to know is that God planned and loved each and every one of us and we can study all of this in very technical, scientific terms but it is God who makes it all possible. He could have chosen any way in the world to make a baby, but He wanted it to be safely tucked inside the mommy. That's why our bodies, boys and girls both, are to be treated with reverence and respect. Each of us is made in God's own image and likeness. We are temples of His Holy Spirit.

Some children may ask but not be ready to hear the answer to "how does the seed get from the father to the mother?" Some are happy with a simple response such as "It happens in bed when the mother and dad are holding each other very tight and the seed passes from the husband to a special place inside the wife."

Other children are ready for details. A short, straightforward reply, offering accurate concise information, is best. Always be careful to assure them that this is part of God's divine plan and is a beautiful and profoundly sacred act that belongs in marriage. For example:

A new baby is created or "conceived" in the mother's womb, when the mommy and daddy are lying very close together in bed. They hug and kiss and hold each other close, as a way of showing how much they love each other. Sometimes when they are alone they will do more than just hug and kiss because their love for each other is so powerful and exciting.

When the man gets excited he becomes aroused, and the seeds that are stored inside of him which can create new life, will pass down through his penis. When he is aroused then, his penis becomes erect and hard.

As the mom and dad lie together, he will place his penis between the mommy's legs where there is an opening called

the vagina. This opening is different from the ones used to uri-
nate or release a bowel movement. The vagina is a special
opening created by God for the penis to fit inside. Once the
penis is inside the vagina, the man's seeds, called "sperm,"
which are carried by a fluid-type substance called "semen," are
released inside the woman.

By the way, this vagina or entryway to the woman's womb
is the same opening that God designed to naturally expand and
enlarge for a pregnant woman to deliver her baby. God thought
of everything and packaged us together beautifully.

Back to the man and woman and how the baby is conceived.
The man's sperm is alive and will then swim around searching for the ovum, or egg. If no egg is present, no baby can be
created.

Now the miracle is, that there are only a few days each
month when the woman's ovum or egg is available and can be
reached by the sperm. For most of the days, some 25 to 28
days, it stays in a little sac up inside the woman and can't be
reached by the sperm. It is the days on which she is "ovulat-
ing," that the woman can become pregnant because the ovum
or egg is ripe and if even one of the man's sperm joins with
it during this special time called "intercourse" a new baby is
created.

There are many technical names used to describe this new
little human being. Each of us began as a "fertilized egg" and
grew quickly as a "zygote" (first six weeks); to an "embryo"
(first two months); to "fetus," which is a Latin term meaning
"young one" or "little one." But even in those very beginning
weeks, you were you!

The preborn baby develops and grows quickly inside the
mother's womb; nature's way of protecting, nurturing and caring for the baby until he or she is ready to be born. The important thing to remember here is that **each and every human
being is created in the image and likeness of God and is
therefore sacred and *always* deserving of our respect.**

**God has a plan and a purpose for each of us and desires
that every little baby before and after birth have a mommy**

and daddy to love and take care of him or her. That is why this "act of love" or intercourse is *only* for a man and woman who are married.

Each act of intercourse is an expression of that married love. A way of saying, "I love you and only you." The baby that may be conceived is really the product or evidence of that powerful love.

"I adjure you, daughters of Jerusalem, by the gazelles and hinds of the field, do not arouse, do not stir up love before its own time" (*Song of Songs* 3:5).

Can We Talk?

(The following is a suggested conversation between parent and young teen.)

Dad: I've been thinking lately about all the pressures coming at teens and you in particular. It must appear that everything revolves around sex.

Jim: Yeah, I guess.

Dad: Most of the things you see, read, or hear about will give you a completely false message about the real beauty and goodness of sex and that its proper place is reserved for marriage.

Jim: What do you mean by "message"?

Dad: I mean that the world out there, Jim, is basically faithless and godless. It often encourages things which are not good. For instance, some very famous people including sports heroes have made headlines by advocating condoms or what they'd like you to believe is "safe sex."

Jim: Yeah, I've seen them. But I already know that's wrong.

Dad: I'm sure you do. Did you know that it's also not as they say "safe"?

Jim: It's supposed to be.

Dad: No son, *anytime* sexual intercourse takes place outside of marriage there is a very real potential for danger. An unmarried couple is risking the chance of getting herpes, which are painful open sores surrounding the genital area. And there is *no* cure. There is also the risk of venereal disease, which can cause permanent damage, including sterility. And of course, there is the risk of AIDS and even death. That doesn't sound very "safe" now does it?

Jim: I guess not. But we never hear of the risks.

Dad: More than all of these reasons, Jim, we want you to know that sex outside of marriage is wrong. It is a serious sin.

Jim: Well, I know you're supposed to be married.

Dad: That's right. God designed sex as a gift to be enjoyed exclusively by a husband and wife in marriage. It's an intimate act reserved for a married couple. This guarantees that if a child is conceived, he or she has loving parents who are committed to each other and to any children God blesses them with. Children need both a mom and a dad and the security of a family. That's why God calls young people to practice chastity, which means to refrain from unlawful sex, before marriage. But all of us are called to a life of chastity.

Jim: How is that?

Dad: God commands Mom and I not to share sexual intimacy or intercourse with anyone else but each other. If we do it is called "adultery." Just like you, we are called to live a life of chastity, being faithful to God and to each other.

Jim: I never thought about it that way.

Dad: Chastity is for everyone. It means to keep ourselves pure, as a gift to God and others. If a married person has sex with someone other than his or her spouse it is called "adultery" and is a serious violation of the sixth commandment. For the unmarried the sin is called "fornication" meaning to have unlawful sex with someone to whom you are not married.

If it is two people of the same sex who engage in unnatural sex acts, the sin is "sodomy" or more commonly known as homosexuality. This is not how God intends us to treat our bodies or others.

Jim: I guess I knew it was wrong. But this does help me understand more clearly.

Dad: And that's exactly why we're talking now, Jim. There are those who may lead you to believe it's old fashioned or almost impossible to wait until marriage. It's not. This is God's law and respecting His commands always lead us to happiness and well being. It's when we sin and break His law that we end up unhappy, disappointing ourselves and others.

Jim: They sure make you think everyone is doing it though.

Dad: Jim, it's not always going to be easy. You will be tempted. Everyone is. You need to know, however, that sins against chastity are serious and can literally work to cut off or block the flow of God's love. It's also selfish and can be a hard habit to break. God has reserved sexual intimacy for married people only. That means that individuals who violate His command by participating in intimate petting, genital touching, or arousal with themselves (called masturbation) or others are saying "No. I will not obey" to God, and "Yes" to their own selfish desires. No matter how exciting it may be at first, it always leads to disappointment, disillusionment, and unhappiness. Once the habit of impurity forms, it becomes stubborn, selfish, and can even ruin the goodness and enjoyment which was meant for the sex act, because it was so habitually misused. After all, God created sexual pleasure for the husband and wife to enjoy to demonstrate their love for each other and as a means to bring new human life into the world. When that gift of sexuality is abused, it always is sinful and can lead to serious misuse. That's why we always want to pray for God's grace; to keep ourselves busy with *good* activities, reading, and friends; and stay away from the occasions which tempt us beyond our means.

Jim: Hmmm.

Dad: Mom and I have great faith in you. We know that it may not always be easy, but we believe in you. We want you to know that if you stay away from those occasions that can weaken your will—such as drinking or drugs or intimate contact and touching on dates, God will always give you the grace necessary to resist. Remember too, Mom and I will be praying for you.

Jim: Thanks, Dad.

Dad: You can be a leader and example of what a real *gentleman* is by treating the young women you know with respect. You can also let the guys in your circle know that you'll have no part of dirty books, videos, behavior, or even "talk" that degrades women or the sacredness the sexual act is intended to be.

Jim: You know how guys like to talk, Dad.

Dad: Yes, I do. But I also know that everyone looks up to and respects a *real* man. We want nothing more than your eternal happiness. **Remember, you will never have to worry about sexually transmitted diseases; pregnancy or having to make an adoption or parenting decision; or the fear, disappointment, and shame that results from such behavior, if you obey God's laws and keep yourself chaste.**

Jim: I believe you, Dad, but I think many of the kids today aren't waiting for marriage. I know some who are messing around. And I'm talking about people you think are "good kids."

Dad: I'm sure you do know some. But that doesn't make it right. God's law is God's law. Sex is reserved for marriage because it is the most profoundly intimate act a man and woman can share. It is meant to be the union of husband and wife in a personal, emotional, spiritual, and physical sense. But it is more than an act of unity. It is something holy. Because of the potential for pregnancy, the Church regards the married couple as "co-creators with God." It is their act of love with God's grace that can bring about the creation of new life. What could be more beautiful and worth waiting for?

Jim: Thanks Dad. I know it's something special and you have helped me understand why.

"So turn from youthful passions and pursue integrity, faith, love, and peace, along with those who call on the Lord in purity of heart" (*Timothy* 2:22).

Grandma D's Breaded Fish Fillet
Terrific for fresh or frozen fillets

Lime or Lemon Juice
1 Egg
1/2 Cup Milk
Flour
1 Cup Bread crumbs
1/2 tsp Accent
1 tsp Salt
1/4 tsp Pepper
1 Tbsp Parsley
1/2 tsp Romano (or Parmesan) Cheese

Rub fish with lemon or lime juice. Season each piece with salt and pepper. Dip fish in flour to coat each side, then dip in slightly beaten egg and milk mixture. Now toss in bread crumb, parsley, accent and cheese mixture, and pan fry in oil, butter or margarine until fish is brown and crispy.

* Even our non-fish lovers like this one. I think the cheese is the secret!

CHAPTER 22

We Can't Pretend Everything Is Okay

"Do not conform yourselves to this age but be transformed by the renewal of your mind, so that you may judge what is God's will, what is good, pleasing and perfect" (*Romans* 12:2).

The issue is a familiar one to most Christian families today. A discussion with four of our children went something like this:

"But, I don't see why we can't go to their place. What's so wrong about that? They come to our house," one of our teens innocently asked.

I tried to explain with an analogy:

"I know this may be difficult, but picture it another way for a moment," I began. "Suppose there is a close relative whom you see and like a great deal and she invites you to her new apartment. When you walk into the living room, you see all new furniture and it's *really* nice. To top it off, you notice in the corners of the room two huge and very expensive stereo speakers. Against one entire wall is a cabinet chuck full of CDs, headphone sets, a tape deck, duo sound amps, the latest in stereo equipment, in addition to a big wide-screen TV."

"Where's this going?" Angie (16) impatiently asked.

"Keep the picture with me," I continued. "When you look out her back window you see she has a cable dish, new yard furniture, and, of course, the apartment complex has a pool.

"In her bedroom is a large canopy poster over a water bed, along with another TV and more stereo equipment.

"And, by the way, it's *all* beautifully decorated. The one drawback. . . ."

"I *figured* something was coming," Mary (18) piped up.

"The one drawback is when she tells you that she regularly shoplifts and confides that some of the neat equipment you've been admiring came from a "fence" whom she regularly trades with. It's stolen goods."

"Yuk!" my expressive teens chimed in unison.

"Now, the question is, 'Would you be comfortable going there to visit again?' "

"No way!" Angie said, speaking for the others. "It wrecks it now that you know."

"Yeah. She took stuff that doesn't belong to her," Kari (14) suggested. "We couldn't go over there after that and pretend that everything is *okay* when it's not!"

"That's right," I said in agreement. "And if you did go back to visit, and even if you tell her that you disapprove of her stealing, your coming to visit and to socialize in her home is helping her live a lie pretending as if stealing is not sinful, when we know that it is. We can never help people feel comfortable or *okay* about serious sin.

"Perhaps now you can better understand why Dad and I feel so strongly about going to the home of two people who are stealing or cheating in another way by living together as if they are husband and wife when they are not married." I explained.

"They are breaking another of God's commandments. It's the Sixth 'Thou shalt not commit adultery,' and no matter how nice and fun a couple may be, and no matter how much we love them and want to be with them, we can't help them financially even if it's just used goods or furniture and we **can't** go over to their place as if everything is in order when we know they are flaunting God's law and living a tremendous lie."

"I got it," Michael (13) added.

"In a way, this couple is also *stealing*," I continued. "They've stolen a gift that is meant to be wrapped and saved

124 Building A Legacy of Love

for marriage; they've stolen each other's virginity and chastity. Each day they live that lie and stay in that unmarried environment, they *steal* something else from each other, the chance to find and be with someone who will **not** use them for sex and temporary companionship, but rather treasure them as a lifetime partner in marriage, as God intends."

"Gosh, I never thought of it that way," Kari said.

"The young man and woman are openly defying God's laws. Marriage is meant to be a lifetime commitment of two, with God as their Third Partner. Sex outside of marriage is a grave sin. It causes shame to the couple; brings scandal to others who see their open defiance; holds the potential for physical health risks such as herpes (which is a lifetime affliction), venereal disease, and AIDS; but sadder still, it involves the very real possibility of placing at risk innocent children who may be conceived from this unstable relationship.

"*Even* the state has laws that protect and uphold matrimony because, as many of our Presidents from Garfield to Reagan have said, 'Marriage and the family are the backbone of society.' The laws are there to safeguard and preserve marriage and to offer stability and security to children.

"Couples who live together outside of marriage are saying, 'Never mind the rules.' Just like the relative who steals, they are saying 'It doesn't belong to us, but we want it *now!*' There are no 'forever' vows as there are in a Sacramental union, and there is no protection or promise of a 'forever family' for any children that result from their togetherness," I explained.

"Well, how about inviting them to our house?" Michael asked.

"Yes. We always want to remind them of our love which we want to be unconditional like God's. Hopefully too, seeing our family will be another reminder of married love and those who try to live in happiness and harmony with God's laws."

This may not be a good idea if the unmarried couple is caustic in attitude; openly boastful about their lifestyle in the presence of small children who may be scandalized; or become demanding, asking to sleep together in the family home.

"I understand better now," Angie confessed. "I thought maybe you were being too 'narrow' about not letting us go there to visit. After all they *are* adults! But I see more clearly since you explained the reasons."

"Thanks for your openness, Angie," I responded.

End of discussion.

So often today, even well meaning people get caught in the trap of **pretending** with family members or friends who are involved in defiant, sinful and perhaps harmful behavior. It's called letting them "do their own thing" and "not passing judgment."

While it is true that only God is the judge, Christians have a very real *responsibility* to 'judge the sin but not the sinner,' to lovingly confront wrongdoers, and to *never* help them to feel comfortable with their sin.

"For merciful and compassionate is the Lord, your God, and He will not turn away His face from you if you return to him" (*2 Chronicles* 30:9).

"Encourage one another daily, while it is still 'today,' so that no one grows hardened by the deceit of sin" (*Hebrews* 3:13).

Mary Ann's (Almost From Scratch) Homemade Pizza

Frozen Bread Dough thawed
8 oz Can Tomato Sauce per pizza
Pepperoni   Italian Sausage
Mozzarella Cheese   Parmesan Cheese
Onion, finely chopped (so the kids can't tell)
   —adds such flavor
Cheddar Cheese
Oregano   Italian spices
Parsley   Fennel seed

   * Options: Hamburger, mushrooms, green peppers, ham, olives (black or green), tuna, variety of cheeses, the ideas are endless.

Take bread dough out and let stand in greased pizza pan (also grease dough so it doesn't crust over). Let rise and then spread out and let it rest for 5 min. before spreading with cooked and cooled sausage (drain off excess fat), pepperoni, spices, onions, cheeses, and whatever your little heart desires (not to mention what any of your finicky eaters will tolerate). My personal trick is to put all the goodies such as mushrooms, onions, black olives etc., in one corner or half of the pan.
   Bake at 425° for 20 minutes and watch to make sure edges don't burn. Set for 3 minutes to cool, cut in pie or square shapes and enjoy.

   * This is a favorite of several priest friends. (I keep making it, but so far no one from this household has announced a priestly vocation!)

CHAPTER 23

Children: Building Them Up As We Raise Them Up

"Virtue guards one who walks honestly, but the downfall of the wicked is sin" (Proverbs 13:6).

"I know one thing for sure," my friend Helen told her ready-for-college daughter. "I don't have to worry about *you* taking drugs or getting into any trouble."

"Why not?" her daughter, Jean, asked in surprise.

"Because you're too smart for that!" Helen declared.

It was years before Helen learned just how significant her words of trust were.

"Mother, you don't know how many times I thought of your words during those years away from home, when I was tempted to get involved in things I knew were wrong," Jean confided one day. "There were *so many* situations with roommates, friends or off-campus parties. But I remembered what you said. I knew you trusted me and I couldn't let you down."

Like most parents, Helen knows confidence and trust in children doesn't just happen, nor is it built on one remark alone.

No, trust and confidence are nurtured like flowers. It begins with a seed, requires nourishment, occasional weeding, loving attention and time. Then comes maturity.

Jean had that maturity and was living up to her parents' expectations.

Child guidance experts agree that **children want and need discipline, structure, and the sense that someone is guiding them. Even when they say they don't.**

Nationally known motivational speaker Zig Ziglar, author of *"Raising Positive Kids in a Negative World,"* says, "Children who are praised for the good things they do, and encouraged in their efforts, will respond positively and are less likely to betray that parental support by getting into serious trouble."

"Conversely," Ziglar says, "psychologists tell us that those children who constantly hear they are "dumb," "stupid" or "can't do *anything* right?" or have no adult in their life who truly cares about them, will do poorly."

It makes sense. It also has much to do with building integrity and a healthy self-esteem.

More than trust, young people *need* moral guidance and principles to live by.

A few years ago the county I live in became a copycat to the City of New York in mandating tax dollars ($65,000 the first year) for the "Clean Needles to Drug Users Program."

Imagine giving people who inject themselves with illegal drugs, clean needles in order that they can do *more* illegal drugs?

Worst of all, such moral "neutrality" miserably fails young people.

On another front, today's adolescents see school officials and authority figures diligent in passing out condoms and contraceptives to teens, yet adamant in preserving a neutrality on morality so as "not to offend non-believers." Thus leaving little room for self-discipline, self-denial, honor, or virtue.

Worst of all such moral "neutrality" miserably fails young people.

Kids are smart. They will live up to what is expected of them.

Little wonder that such medical journals as *Emergency Medicine,* and others routinely feature articles on the rise and risk of sexually transmitted diseases occurring in young people, revealing that some adolescents who experimented with sex now face incurable diseases such as herpes, VD, AIDS and an early death. All because they "didn't think it could happen to me."

Young people need to be told about chastity, and that waiting until marriage is the right thing to do.

They also deserve to know the truth: **There is no such thing as *safe* or *safer* sex when it occurs outside of a faithful married state.**

What a contrast and contradiction to the Holy Father, Pope John Paul II, who spoke to 160,000 young people at Cherry Creek State Park in the Colorado Rockies; as well as to millions of others on his trips to Canada, Africa, and the Philippines. His message is the same:

So much depends on you!. . . The church needs your energies, your enthusiasm, your youthful ideals, in order to make the Gospel of Life penetrate the fabric of society, transforming people's hearts and the structures of society in order to create a civilization of true justice and love. Now more than ever, in a world that is often without light and without the courage of noble ideals, people need the fresh, vital spirituality of the Gospel.

Pope John Paul II believes in young people. "I came [to see the Pope]," one young man told a curious reporter, "because he holds up standards to believe in and live by." Yes, children occasionally fail, just like adults, but they will work very hard to win the approval of those they admire, love and respect. What can parents, do? We can begin with prayer for God's grace and guidance.

Next, we can be consistent in guiding, loving, and most importantly, encouraging our young. Here are a few things we've learned along the way:

• **Cheerlead and compliment.** Children are more anxious to please their parents and loved ones than anyone else. Let's not let them down. We want them to know that whether they're on the court or in the trenches, we're rooting for them. *We* think they are the **greatest.**

• **Applaud accomplishments.** Achievements large and small may long be forgotten, but the applause, affection, hugs, and the "I love you and I'm proud of you" will endure and work to build a child's self-esteem like no classroom instruction ever could.

• **Trust them with tasks.** Doing a job well builds character, confidence, and trust. Even very young children want to feel needed and a part of something. A lesson learned anew the year we adopted Charlie, a six year-old from Vietnam. Seeing all of us busy with routine Saturday chores, and not knowing any English to express himself, he grabbed the vacuum from his brother, Tim, refusing to let him do his work.

"Mom, help me. He won't let go of the vacuum," Tim cried.

"Let's see if he would like to sweep the kitchen floor with a broom instead," I responded. You guessed it. As soon as I offered the broom, Charlie grinned his toothless smile and went eagerly to do *his* task. He now felt a part of our family. And isn't that what adoption and family life is all about?

• **Care enough to check.** Children, including adolescents and young adults, need to feel our watchful, guiding, *presence*.

Off limits are: parties without parents, at-home dates without supervision, under age drinking, co-ed camping, motel prom nights or even unsupervised pajama parties where a parent doesn't occasionally poke a head in and say "Just checking to see if you kids need anything."

Children need to know we're there for them, prodding, praying, and prompting their goodness even when they wish we weren't. They can thank us later!

• **Don't overload or over-estimate.** Rights go with responsibilities. Privileges, such as extended curfews, dating, or attending special events, etc., will occur as youngsters grow in age and trust. We fail them miserably when we say, "You're old enough to set your own limits, make your own choices, decision, etc." After all, we are the parents and possess far more experience and knowledge about what can happen or go wrong than an impetuous youth who only sees the here and now.

To build self-esteem, let's tell our young:

• **You can do most anything if you work hard, pray for God's guidance, and treat others respectfully.**

• **Do what is right. God will help you. Just ask Him.**

"Observe what is right, do what is just. . .All who keep the Sabbath. . . and hold to my covenant, them I will bring to my holy mountain and make joyful in my house. . . ." (*Isaiah* 56:1-7).

• **"If at first you don't succeed try try again!" Don't be a quitter and *always* do your best.** Failure is not *trying*.

• **Be a person of good moral character.** A good rule of thumb was given by Congressman J.C. Watts, Jr. (R-Oklahoma) in his speech at the l996 Republican National Convention. Watts, a 31 year-old black man and former football quarterback, who told of "growing up on the wrong side of the tracks in a poor family," said; **"Character is doing what's right when nobody's watching!"**

• **Plan ahead. Set some *realistic* goals.** Some people never get anywhere in life, because they really don't know where they are headed. Ask yourself, "What do I like to do? Where would I like to be 5 or 10 years from now? How can I get there?"

• **Find something you like to do and stick with it!** Even things we enjoy doing require discipline and effort. Look at the great inventors, artists, athletes, composers, historical figures, and world leaders. *All* of them overcame great challenges before success.

• **Opposition offers opportunity.** Opposition and adversity strengthen our determination and discipline.

St. Paul writes, *"Goodness comes from all things for those who love the Lord"* (*Romans* 8:28). Ask God to help you see the goodness.

• **Copycats are never as happy as "trail blazers."** Don't be afraid to be creative and *never* do something just because a friend does, unless it is a project or task you want to do, or feel will be of service to another.

• **Look to your loved ones.** Friends are fickle, acquaintances are casual, but family and loved ones are *unconditional*. Always remember your parents are pulling for you. They want what's best for you and will help you.

• **Be a "cheerful cheerleader."** The more you encourage

and applaud the accomplishments of others, the more they are eager to help you in your own achievements. Character has little to do with selfishness or self-centeredness.

• **Dream a little.** What do you find fulfilling, fun, and productive? Ask God to help you work on the creative tools he gave you. Remember, He has a plan for you.

"Before I formed you in the womb I knew you, and before you were born I consecrated you" (*Jeremiah* 1:5).

• **Be grateful.** You are the child of a loving God who created a mission just for you. Look around at all He has given you. Have you thanked Him today? Ask Him how you can use your talents and abilities to serve others.

In a world of pessimism and negative solutions to real problems, let us never forget that as Christians we know the answer, Jesus.

"You are the light of the world. . . . Let your light shine before men so that they may see goodness in your acts and give praise to your heavenly Father" (*Matthew* 5:14-16).

Chrissy's Strawberry Jello Salad
A sure hit with even the fussiest of kids

3 sm pkg (4 oz) Strawberry Jello (or 2 lg pkg)
1 frozen (10 oz) Cool Whip
1 frozen (10 oz) pkg Strawberries

Follow Jello instructions using only <u>one</u> cup cold water. Add frozen strawberries and let set. Mix Cool Whip in Strawberry Jello with hand mixer.

Cool and serve.

CHAPTER 24

Getting Rid Of The Mice

"He who loves his son chastises him often, that he may be his joy when he grows up" (*Sirach* 30:1).

I've just lived through one of the worst ordeals. At least for this week. I couldn't eat, sleep, or concentrate. We had a mouse in the house!

Now mind you, I've always prided myself in being a pretty tidy homemaker and that includes the kids' rooms which must pass weekly inspection and my "clean room test." Or there's "grounding" and a fine to be paid (commensurate with the age).

So how did the mouse get in the house? The pest control man tried to be reassuring, suggesting it was "the nearby construction a few doors down, the colder weather, or merely a door left open" more than likely in this busy household and with six kids still at home.

"It's either me or the mouse!" I told the man.

My husband, John, wanted to know if I was moving. Always the tease, he kept asking the kids, "Has anyone seen Mickey today? Let's get his autograph!"

I was in no mood to joke. And it sure didn't help to know our gradeschoolers told all their friends on the playground about "Mickey." So much for dignity.

"How can something so little cause so much disruption?" I asked, before I caught myself. How could a mother of 13 even ask such a question.

Eventually our lives resumed to "normalcy" (whatever that is) after Roger from the pest control agency helped get rid of "Mickey."

Getting rid of an intruder or unwelcome guests, whether it's mice, lice, infection, or simply the common cold, is a good reminder of the lengths moms and dads will go to in order to protect their children from unhealthy or negative situations.

We want our children to be in a clean, safe, and loving environment, surrounded by good things which will strengthen them in body and soul.

Hopefully, the same zeal applies to issues that affect our children's souls.

Unfortunately today, there are those who suggest that when youngsters reach a certain age, even while living at home, they can decide for themselves what type of reading, listening, or viewing material is "right for them."

Deuteronomy is another reminder to parents: *"Take care and be earnestly on your guard not to forget the things which your own eyes have seen, nor let them slip from your memory as long as you live, but teach them to your children and to your children's children"* (*Deuteronomy* 4:9-10).

After all, it is our experience, expertise, example and insight, that our own young rely and depend on.

On occasion, however, and just like the mouse, I have had to rid our home of undesirable movies, music, and magazines. I don't think twice. If it's on my property and John and I believe the material is offensive—it's history.

I've thrown out "Top Ten" *artists* I use the term loosely. I've tossed cassettes, and I've scratched across CDs, to make absolutely sure another innocent adolescent isn't influenced.

Once I found a Madonna video under a 20 year-old's bed. She tried every argument including the one "But Mom, she's Christian!" Oh Yeah?

One son subscribed to a hot rod magazine. "What could be healthier than that and tinkering with old cars?" I thought. Until I saw its "swimsuit edition." Luckily, there was a razor blade on hand and every model and centerfold was lifted before he came home from college. I told him I saved the best part of the hotrods for him to see without *distraction!* The subscription was canceled.

Kids are very innocent and really don't want to be involved with indecent or offensive material. However, they are also very curious, and once exposed to the suggestive or sinful, it can become habit forming. Parents must be prepared to offer guidance and in some cases, lay down the law.

I believe a mother can almost *sense* when a child has become influenced by obscene or cultist material. It can even come in the form of comic books. Trust me.

I'll never forget the time I found a pile of satanic comic books in one of my sons' closets while hunting for a little one's missing shoe.

One of the stories actually depicted the heroine devouring, for "strength," the bodies of "newborn babies," much like Popeye ate spinach.

My teenage son had *no idea.* He had picked up a sackful of the books after cashing his paycheck from his part-time job at the ice cream shop. He thought they were a new *action* series. Out they went! An expensive lesson for him and a warning to this mom: not even comic books are safe.

I told him it was his Guardian Angel always acting as protector who led me to the offensive comics.

Once I found the lyrics to a New Age song which advocated an obvious devotion to crystals and "readings," in one of my daughter's rooms. A good opportunity to tell her about cults, fads, and fortune telling. She had no idea and was only attracted by the catchy tune. I believe her.

Children, including young adults, may be totally unaware of the nature or hidden meaning of the lyrics or words playing to them. In fact, they may not be consciously listening.

Another time, I found a compact disk with lyrics depicting violence with messages and sarcastic innuendoes against Christianity and those who follow Christ!

When I read it out loud to my two boys, they both sat stunned with dropped jaws. "Honestly Mom, we had no idea it was bad. We bought it for one song and this other stuff was on it." I believe them.

Moms and Dads can't be bullied by the size and age of a child still living at home. I remember my friend Carol who confided to several of us one day while working at a church function, "What do you do when your boys bring home rented tapes that are R rated? I just hate it! Some are so violent and really portray women in a demeaning way. But, I feel I can't say anything any more, because they're big guys now sixteen and nineteen year-olds. By that age I feel they have some rights."

"So do I," our friend, Meg, responded, "But if it's in your house, Carol, and you don't approve, it must go. After all, it's your home, your equipment, and ultimately it will be you who condones the material no matter what you *say* if it is permitted."

Carol was grateful for the frank advice. It gave her courage to talk to her sons: "I've made a mistake in the past by allow- ing you to bring home music and videos of which I disapprove. But no more. If it goes against my Catholic faith or morals, it's out! I want our home to be a loving Christian environ- ment." Her sons balked at first, and they did test the rule once or twice, but they did comply.

Seven of our children are now grown and on their own. Through the years, I've come to believe our "off-limits" pol- icy on material we feel is offensive has brought more peace and serenity than the few occasional hassles we've had with a teen or young adult who wants to "make up my own mind."

As parents we're not here to win a popularity contest. We're here as protectors and guides to help get our children to their goal—Heaven.

Ultimately, we are responsible, and not our young no mat- ter the age for what is allowed in our home. "Someday we will have to answer to our Heavenly Father for the kinds of enter- tainment we exposed our kids to. I have enough to answer for as it is!"

The mouse episode reminded me of how easily things can

creep into our homes, invade our peace of mind, and cause a disturbance. Indecent or vulgar material has the same effect.

In a manner of speaking, parents are "God's Pest Control Agents!"

"Finally, my brothers, your thoughts should be wholly directed to all that is true, all that deserves respect, all that is honest, pure, admirable, decent, virtuous, or worthy of praise" (*Philippians* 4:8).

Crab Stuffed Potatoes
A dinner party favorite

4 Potatoes, flat & oblong
1/4 Cup Butter
1/2 Cup light Cream
1 tsp Salt
5 tsp Onion (grated)
1/2 Cup Cheddar Cheese (or you can mix in a little Swiss for flavor)
1/2 tsp Paprika
1 6 oz Can Crabmeat

Scrub potatoes. Bake at 325° for 30 minutes then pierce potatoes with fork to allow steam to escape and make potatoes mealy and dry. Continue baking (about another 30 min). While potatoes are baking, drain crabmeat (if necessary, remove any cartilage). Now cut potatoes in half, lengthwise. Scoop out potato inside and whip with butter by hand or electric mixer. Add all ingredients, except crabmeat and paprika. With a fork, mix in the crabmeat lightly. Refill potato shells. Lightly pile up the filling. Sprinkle with paprika and re-heat in hot oven at 450° for 15 minutes. Serve hot.

CHAPTER 25

If There's A Mother Out There
Praying—Watch Out Kids!

"Because you have the Lord for your refuge; you have made the Most High your stronghold. No evil shall befall you, nor shall affliction come near your tent, For to His angels he has given command about you, that they guard you in all your ways" (*Psalm* 91:9-11).

"I suppose all your kids are perfect and you don't have any trouble spots in the pack," my friend blurted out.

"Hardly!" I quickly assured her.

"In fact, when you have as many as I do, everything seems to come in twos! Two of our kids might be getting awards or enjoying the limelight, while the behavior of two others is robbing my concentration and absorbing my prayers. I suppose you could say, it helps keep my balance. It also does wonders for my prayer life, not to mention the opportunity for humility."

"Thank heavens!" my friend sighed. "I was almost afraid to ask."

And that's just one of the reasons it's good for moms to get together.

Fathers may not need the socialization and camaraderie that mothers do, but speaking as a "seasoned Mom," I believe that taking "time out" to share with others, whether it's over cof-

138

fee, lunch, or the telephone (not nearly as much fun but does help especially on days when we're snowed in or quarantined with sick kids), can be supportive and downright rejuvenating.

Just being able to tell another mother about an everyday fear or frustration, seems to lessen its hold. Problems may not always be solved but just hearing someone say, "I know what you mean," "I've been there myself," or even, "I can't imagine how you must feel but I'll be praying," can carry us through for hours, if not days.

On the really down days—and we all have them—what helps most is having Christian friends who remind us that "God is in control even when we are not."

Thank heavens!

After lunch with a good friend, and a few laughs (always the best medicine), I'm usually ready to roll up my sleeves and head for the laundry room to tackle one more dirty load or worse yet, clean Dominic's closet!

If there's one old adage that always sent shivers up my back, it was, "Little children, little troubles; bigger children, bigger problems."

Thanks a lot! What's a mom to do? Shelve them in a deep freeze from 13 to 19?

What couple in their right mind would ever want to have children with *that* to look forward to? Oh what anxiety we heap on such novice souls.

Lucky for me, I knew several more experienced moms who saw every age and every stage as both gift and challenge. My friend, Mary, a mother of four boys, who had gone through most of their teen years when we first met, was more than encouraging and supportive. "Don't listen to those old tales. You'll make it, kid!" she'd counsel.

Mary was right. Before I realized it, we had six teens at once, with seven more to come. Our household took on a new kind of atmosphere. I'm not talking about the heaps of dirty socks, smelly tennis shoes, or the persistent odor of shampoo and hair spray. That's a given.

No. I'm talking about the breath of new life that comes with a teenager's moods, music, and manner. There's nothing like viewing the world anew through the eyes of one who is not weighted down with experience, logic, or caution.

It's prudence to the winds, only to be tamed and tempered by the loving discipline of a "remote control" maturity we lovingly know as *parents.*

There is no age group more impetuous, idealistic, and imaginative than teens. They bring a vibrancy and vision like no toddler could. Hair raising and unpredictable at times, I would not have it any other way.

My teens have brought me up to date, kept me current, and forced a futuristic look at society that may have left me standing at the kitchen sink were it not for them dragging me into the nineties and beyond whether I'm ready or not.

All in all, and speaking from "survivor experience," children of all ages from tots to teens and beyond are *pure gift* and truly blessings to the vocational call of parenthood.

That's not to say I appreciate all the experimenting with fashion, fads, impulses, or ideas. And yes, there've been times we've worried, and other times when we've pulled in the reigns to prevent and to protect them. It's called LOVE.

"So, when do we quit worrying?" another Mom once jokingly asked over lunch. "Never," I've resolved.

My friend, Pat, once confided, "I remember breathing the biggest sigh of relief when our firstborn walked down the aisle to receive his high school diploma. I figured, he's 18 and graduated. My worries are over. I didn't realize that I would *always* be praying and *always* be concerned even if from a distance."

That's what parenting is all about.

For well over a decade I belonged to a prayer group. Most of us were housewives and mothers who gathered weekly to pray for our families and, in particular, our children. The Blessed Mother and our childrens' patron saints were often sought as helpmates.

Fortunately, Catholics can rely on a whole arsenal of saints, our "friends in high places" to pray with us for our children.

My kids say I'm "sneaky."

Maybe so, but it works.

Recently, my son, Tony, was home on leave from the Army and confided to a brother, "It was pretty tempting to mess around like some of the other guys, but remembering Mom kind of wrecks it for ya. I knew she was praying."

How's that for *long distance?*

Our children may still make mistakes, commit sin, hurt themselves and others, and in some cases we may not see a turn around in their disappointing behavior in our own lifetime.

That doesn't mean we quit praying. After all, we are people of faith and you know what they say about "mothers who pray!"

Here are some of my favorite Saints. They always seem to hear a mother's prayer:

• **The Blessed Mother:** Who more than Mary, Our Mother, would have Christ's ear and plead our case?

• **St. Anne:** "Patronness of Housewives," Anne is the mother of Mary and grandmother of Jesus.

• **Your child's Patron Saint:** Be assured that this Saint, when asked, will join in prayer for the child who is his or her namesake.

• **St. Michael the Archangel:** Known as the most powerful of the angels, Michael is a forceful protector against bodily or spiritual harm.

• **Your child's Guardian Angel:** Each of us has our own special Guardian Angel. Parents can pray daily to their child's angel, that he or she be guarded and protected from undue temptation or trial.

• **St. Maria Goretti:** Canonized by Pope Pius XII (1950) for her purity. Eleven-year-old Maria was killed by a would-be rapist whom she forgave. St. Maria is a beautiful model for young people.

• **St. Anthony:** "Patron Saint of Lost Articles" and also of "Travelers." Surely this saint will watch over our mobile children, and also the ones who stray or occasionally seem to lose their way.

• **St. Rita:** "Patron Saint of the Impossible" and desperate situations! Married against her will, this saint endured cruelty and hardship yet remained a shining example of faith to others.

• **St. Monica:** "Patron of Mothers," Saint Monica prayed for her pagan son, Augustine, for 39 years. Once converted, he became Bishop of Hippo and one of the greatest theologians of the Church.

• **St. Therese of Lisieux:** Nicknamed the "Little Flower" Therese died at the age of 24. A cloistered Carmelite nun, she called her prayerlife "the little way" and promised that after her death she would spend her life in Heaven doing good for those on earth. St. Therese is one of my special "Heavenly friends!"

• **St. Gerard:** "Patron of Expectant Mothers," Saint Gerard Majella an Italian Redemptorist lay brother, is the favorite of millions who seek intercessory prayer for pregnancy and safe delivery. My daughter, Chrissy has a special devotion to St. Gerard in thanksgiving for her first daughter, Elizabeth Marie.

Italian Marinated Salad
Great for parties, showers, luncheons or picnics

1 lg head Cauliflower
4 bunch Broccoli flower
1 lb fresh Mushroom, sliced
2 bunch Red Radish, cut up
2 Green Peppers, sliced
1 Red Onion, sliced in rings
Cherry Tomatoes, basket
1 lg can pitted ripe Olives
2 cans marinated Artichoke Hearts (don't drain)
1 lg Seven Seas Italian Dressing
1 jar Olive Candite
Mozzarella or Cheddar Cheese, sliced thin

Clean vegetables, mix together with salad dressing in large bowl and store in refrigerator. Stir occasionally. Just before serving add one jar of Progresso (or any brand of Olive Candite, not drained). Enjoy! This can be made the night before.

* Or, you can cheat a little, skip the Candite and use your own favorite Italian salad dressing.

CHAPTER 26

God's Forgiveness—Always Near And Never Long Distance

"We implore you, in Christ's name: be reconciled to God!" (*2 Corinthians* 5:20).

My son, Tony called home the other day from his new assignment in Fort Hood, Texas. As always, our cordless phone (marvelous invention) is passed around to every family member, including those playing basketball in the backyard.

Each gives a report on the latest happenings, which can be anything from: Michael (12) taking "second in baseball play-offs," Dominic (10) beginning trumpet lessons, Angie (15) and Kari (14) learning to sew (Mom's happy), to Joseph (7) having a birthday and losing another tooth.

Finally, it's my turn. After offering my own "news notes," i.e.: Grandma's feeling better, Charlie likes his new job in Colorado, Mary (18) leaves for college in September, and did you get my last letter?; I get to the topics most good mothers of a far-away child want to know:

"So, have you met anyone special since you were transferred to Texas?" I begin.

"Not really," he responds. (I'm never quite sure if that's good or bad.)

"Well what do you do on your off time?" I probe.

"Just hang with the guys, shoot some hoops, 'work out' (you

would think he gets enough as an Army Infantryman), or scope the nearby towns" (meaning "looks around for girls").

"Hmmm," I thoughtfully reply. "Well how about the church?" (He knew it was coming.) "Where do you go for Mass on Sunday?" (Notice the finesse and how I just *assume.*)

"Don't worry Ma, I'm going. Actually I don't know the priest's name but it's a nice church although I still miss St. Charles."

"Well how about Confession? Don't stay away just because you don't know the priests or aren't as comfortable there."

By now he's chuckling. "I knew you'd get around to it! Somehow, you always work it in!"

"Good," I respond. "At least I'm not disappointing you. I wouldn't be your Mom if I didn't check out your spiritual side and make sure everything is okay and in order."

"Yeah I know. That's my Mom!" Tony laughingly replies.

"The Mass is central to our Faith," I remind him. "And, the Eucharist is Christ's ongoing gift to us. But, Reconciliation helps our souls stay in shape so that we can receive this gift. We're so blessed to have this Sacrament."

Capturing how most Catholics feel about Confession, Tony said, "I have to admit, I don't look forward to it. I even try to postpone or avoid going. But you know something? When I do get around to going, the minute I walk out of that Confessional I feel *sooo* good. It's something you can't even explain."

Music to mom's ears!

When you think about it, God could have chosen any way He wanted to forgive sin, but He chose His Apostles and their successors, the Bishops, and the priests ordained by them, to convey this sacrament.

Christ's words were clear: *"Receive the Holy Spirit; whose sins you shall forgive, they are forgiven them; and whose sins you shall retain, they are retained"* (*John* 20:22-23).

As parents, we want our kids to know that ultimately it is not the priest who hears and forgives our sins, but Christ Himself, who uses the ears, lips, hands, and human body of the priest to transmit His forgiveness and grace to us. For our part, all we need do is confess our sins, be truly sorry, and sincerely *intend* to avoid that sin in the future.

Many Catholics feel as Tony does and approach the confessional with sweaty palms and perhaps a healthy humility and fear. The sense of relief and peace of mind that comes the instant absolution is given, however, is as Tony says, "impossible to explain."

Reconciliation is a wonderful and powerful Sacrament. Yet, it is so often neglected. Unfortunately today, there is much talk about love but little of guilt and shame, or sorrow for sin. Society, in fact, has lost its sense of sin.

According to the *Catholic Catechism,* sin is nothing short of "an offense against God and a rupture of communion with Him." Confession, it says, offers a *conversion* because it is "the first step in returning to the Father from whom one has strayed by sin. In a profound sense it is an "acknowledgment and praise of the holiness of God and of His mercy toward sinful man" (p. 327, #1423).

"Think of Confession like Popeye's spinach," I tell my younger children. "In the cartoons when he's weak and nearly beaten, he gulps down that can of spinach and is **instantly transformed with power and might."**

"Going to Confession is even more powerful. It unloads those sins, lifts a weight off your spirit, brings you closer to God, and **gives you spiritual ammunition, Sanctifying Grace to help you fight off temptation. How's that for** *power?"*

After all, God wants us to be happy. He does not want us to be dragged down by sin. (At times it might feel lighter dragging around a dead horse.)

Scripture reminds us, *"Hence, declare your sins to one another, and pray for one another, that you may find healing"* (*James* 5:16).

When you think of it, thousands of dollars are spent every day by non-believers for psychiatrists and therapists, in an effort to relieve guilt and obtain that elusive peace of mind.

Catholics, on the other hand, have the counsel of priests, the confidentiality of the confessional, and the healing grace that comes through the Sacrament of Reconciliation. I'd say that's a peace of mind money can't buy.

We can't remind our children often enough that God loves them. His forgiveness is ever present and *knows no bounds.* We want them to know that His love flows constantly no matter what we do. Our sins, however, are obstacles to that flow; and serious (mortal) sin stops it from getting through to our hearts altogether.

The seriousness of sin must never be diminished. To diminsh sin, would diminish the Cross and the very reason Christ suffered and died for us. In fact, He went to the cross as if we were the only one in the world in need of His redemptive love.

Scripture says: *"If you live according to the flesh you will die; but if by the spirit you put to death the evil deeds of the body, you will live"* (*Romans* 8:12).

Reconciliation offers forgiveness and keeps that current of grace flowing to us.

Parents need this Sacrament, too. And what better example to our children. "It's been a while and about time we *all* go!" I periodically tell our young.

We were young once ourselves (my children doubt it) and oftentimes it was the gentle nudge of someone who loved us that reminded us that God is near, in fact, he's as close as the nearest confessional!

"Faith in the heart leads to justification, confession on the lips to salvation" (*Romans* 10:9-10).

Filippino Dinner
So easy

Round Steak
Vegetables, chopped (celery, carrots, onions, broccoli, green
    pepper, mushrooms, zucchini)
Lemon Juice
3 Tbsp Soy Sauce
1 Tbsp Cornstarch
2 pkgs Raman Soup

Mix Soy Sauce and cornstarch. Cut steak into bite size
pieces, pour sauce over and marinate meat for three hours (or
more). Stir fry meat, then add assorted vegetables (feel free to
add water chestnuts, bean sprouts and whatever else your family won't pick out of the meal). Cook noodles in separate pan.
Drain. Add Raman season mix to meat mixture, lemon juice
over top. Then just before serving add Raman noodles over top
and serve. It looks like you've concocted something special!

CHAPTER 27

I'm Grateful For Single People

"For you are my hope, O Lord; my trust, O God, from my youth. On You I depend from birth; from my mother's womb You are my strength; constant has been my hope in You" (*Psalm* 71:5-6).

This is one Mom who is downright grateful for the single people in my kids' lives.

Most parents discover early on that children learn not by word, but by *osmosis*. They are continually observing and "picking up" behavior from those around them and that includes their unmarried brothers and sisters, aunts and uncles, teachers, advisors, neighbors, and family friends.

The single Christians in our midst who consciously live their lives as God calls them to live are helping to dispel the myth of immorality and are examples we parents can point to and ones our children can look up to. They are part of God's plan in helping to build up his "Domestic Church."

"Tell those who are rich in this world's goods . . .not to rely on so uncertain a thing as wealth . . . . Charge them to do good, to be rich in good works and generous, sharing what they have. Thus will they build a secure foundation for the future, for receiving that life which is life indeed" (*1 Timothy* 6:17-19).

Lets face it, participating in youth and church programs may come more naturally to many parents. After all, our children are, or will be, benefiting from these endeavors. Thus, we gladly sign up to coach, chaperone, lead, or teach.

But what of those individuals who have no children, yet use their time and talent, not to mention that ingredient most stretched parents lack *energy* to be of service to others? Often they are the "unsung heroes!"

To those men and women Scripture promises, *"God loves a cheerful giver"* (2 *Corinthians* 9:7).

A good example, is my daughter Mary's recent experience of going on a TEC (To Encounter Christ) weekend retreat. As a busy high school senior with a part-time job, preparation for college, and precious little free time with her own friends, the idea of attending a weekend retreat was admittedly not on the top of her list. But she went at our urging.

"What was really nice, was just being with a whole roomful of people whose beliefs were like mine," she later recalled. It didn't hurt either to know that most of the TEC leaders were young, single adults.

The church, missions, youth interests, and pro-life concerns are just some of the areas that benefit from the sacrifices made by single Christian men and women committed to bringing the Good News to others.

Even more, as a mom of many, I know what a profound difference it can make to send a teen, especially one who has reached the age of "know-it-all," (a couple of ours once fit this description) into a campsite, classroom, or basketball court, and be confronted by a single adult who has no qualms about openly embracing his faith or being of service to church and community.

"My kids may think they've 'heard it all before,' but when they see vibrant young adults like you who openly talk about your faith and fidelity to God's laws they *are impressed!*" I recently told a group of single CCD teachers after their evening classes.

I believe that goodness works like a magnet, drawing others to it.

But, Christian single adults do more than take our kids

camping, coach their games, or serve as instructors and counselors. They are our moral echoes as they quietly live their faith and fundamental values.

They are helping our kids, and countless others, visualize virtue rather than vice. And, this mom *is* grateful!

But more than the moral authority and activism, I am also thankful for the *mere presence* of good Christian single men and women within our families and communities.

What a contrast they are to a world which gives constant recognition to the self-absorbed and self-centered. Even the word bachelor brings to mind images of unchecked luxury and lustful living. Yet, here are these individuals striving to lead morally good lives. A profound and welcome witness.

Self-control and self-denial are their standards not sin!

Single people young and old are part of God's plan to help to strengthen and build up his "Domestic Church."

Every Christian parent prays their own children will one day grow up to become "Christ-like" role models and mentors, no matter their vocational call to others.

"It gives me great joy to see my college-age sons coaching sports at St. Charles" Dr. Gasik, a family physician, confided during a recent visit. "When they were young and students themselves I used to tell them, 'So much has been given to you. When you get older I hope you will turn around and give some of what you have received to others.' To see them spending their free time like this is very gratifying."

Rightly so and *Bravo!*

Being of service to others may come a bit more naturally to the married or those living in the religious life. Single people, on the other hand, must *go out of their way* to practice self-denial and to care for the needs of others.

All Christian parents are called to encourage their children and to direct their youthful energy and volunteerism, helping to keep them headed heavenward. As moral guides, we want to remind our young to ask themselves often:

• *"How does God call me to live?"*

• *"How can I use my time, talent, and energy to be of service to Christ, my family, and community?"*

John Paul II said it best.

"Like Mary, you must not be afraid to allow the Holy Spirit to help you become intimate friends of Christ. Like Mary, you must put aside any fear, in order to take Christ to the world in whatever you do—in marriage, as single people in the world, as students, as workers, as professional people. Christ wants to go to many places in the world and to enter many hearts through you. Just as Mary visited Elizabeth, so you too are called to 'visit' the needs of the poor, the hungry, the homeless, those who are alone or ill; for example, those suffering from AIDS. You are called to *stand up* for life, to respect and defend the mystery of life always and everywhere, including the lives of unborn babies, giving real help and encouragement to mothers in difficult situations. You are called to work and pray against abortion, against violence of all kinds, including the violence done against women's and children's dignity through pornography. *Stand up* for the life of the aged and the handicapped, against attempts to promote assisted suicide and euthanasia. *Stand up* for marriage and family life! *Stand up* for purity!" (Oct. 7, 95. Central Park Mass, U.S. Papal Visit).

The next time you see a single person living as God calls them to live and doing something special for someone else, give 'em a "bear hug" and "thank you." Aren't you glad they're there?

"Brothers, I beg you through the mercy of God to offer your bodies as a living sacrifice, holy and acceptable to God. Do not conform yourselves to this age, but be transformed" (*Romans* 12:1-2).

Grasshopper Pie
For that special occasion

24 Cream filled Chocolate Cookies, finely crushed (use blender to crush)
1/4 Cup Margarine, melted
1/4 Cup Milk
Few drops Peppermint Extract
Green Food Coloring
1 Jar Kraft Marshmallow Creme
2 Cup Heavy Cream, whipped

Combine cookie crumbs and margarine. Press into a 9 inch spring pan, reserving 1/2 cup of mixture for topping. Gradually add milk, extract and food coloring to marshmallow creme, mixing until well blended. Fold in whipped cream, pour into pan. Sprinkle with remaining crumbs. Then freeze. Makes 8 to 10 servings.

* If desired substitute 1/4 cup green Creme de Menthe for milk. Omit Peppermint extract and coloring.

* We served this for Tim's Grooms Dinner which was 60 people at our house! I couldn't have done it without my friends the Archambaults, Flemings, and Kelly's, who served as our hostesses! God is good.

CHAPTER 28

Marriage—Opposites Make It With Faith!

"Happy the husband of a good wife, twice-lengthened are his days;

A worthy wife brings joy to her husband, peaceful and full is his life.

A good wife is a generous gift bestowed upon him who fears the Lord;

Be he rich or poor, his heart is content, and a smile is ever on his face"

(*Sirach* 26:1-4).

I admit it. My husband, John, does the major grocery shopping at our house and am I ever grateful. Keeping track of all those coupons and little cut-outs makes me nervous.

We're quite the Odd Couple to some, I suppose. Many an evening we can be seen at opposite ends of the kitchen table. There's John, painstakingly sorting his coupons and special offers, while I sit at the other end, feverishly writing some editorial or commentary more likely to be rejected than published.

"There's my Little Honey," John says, "so busy trying to save the nation, while I'm trying to feed the family."

And so it goes. Yet, as he tells the kids, "We can't afford to let Mom in a grocery store every week. She picks up everything in sight and forgets to look at the price."

I can't help myself. It all looks so good!

Okay so my forté is *not* grocery shopping. John says he's

preserving my energy for other things, like cooking and cleaning, teaching our teens to drive (his patience wears thin), and telling the kids about the facts of life and sex.

What a guy!

In a family our size, we not only face a host of birthdays each one deserving special recognition and celebration, of course, but we often seem to double up on other noteworthy events as well. Take the Spring of 1996, when we experienced no less than two graduations (Mary, high school; Kari, eighth grade); Joseph's First Holy Communion; Kari's Confirmation; and the Wedding of our firstborn son, Tim.

And it all occurred within weeks of each other. Was I busy! Part of it was doing what I enjoy most, bargain hunting and "power shopping," (as the kids would say) coordinating outfits for each event and family member.

Each of these occasions brings a blessing of its own. Yet, there's something about a wedding celebration that brings family and friends together from near and far.

When Tim found Tina, the girl of his dreams and a young lady we all fell in love with, she was an answer to more than just *his* prayers.

Let's be honest, *most* Christian parents continue to pray for their young no matter their age and we are especially thankful when the spouse they choose to marry shares their faith and fundamental values, as Tim and Tina do. With six children still at home, it's also a wonderful example to those still coming up the ranks.

Does faith and similar values matter? In my view, it not only matters, but can mean the difference between a marriage that makes it and one that does not. An exaggeration? Consider the chance a marriage has if one spouse believes in total fidelity and a lifetime commitment but is united to one who has little knowledge or respect for faithfulness in marriage or a resolve to stick it out "for better for worse, in sickness and in health, till death do us part." Winning the lottery may be easier.

Certainly, all married couples face temptation, trials, and a testing of their love. It's part of life. But, each time the "bail

out" of divorce is rejected and a commitment to marriage is
renewed, God's grace flows. In fact, God promises all the
grace necessary for any situation if we but ask!

Yet, for the one who shares no vision of God and His power
to bless and sustain, such trials can be overwhelming. How do
they survive crisis, addictions, or issues involving money, children (their schooling and religious upbringing) as well as a
host of other challenges?

Most people reflect the values and beliefs of their parents.
It's what they've seen and know best. If those parents believed
in commitment and the foreverness of a vow; if they saw children not as a commodity but as a blessing to be welcomed and
cherished; if they saw marriage not as a "fifty-fifty proposi-
tion," but as a vocation worthy of their giving *one hundred
percent* so too will their children. This may not guarantee success, but we know the opposite insures failure.

You bet, we Christian parents pray for our children's future
decisions and the choices they make.

It is no coincidence that Jesus chose the wedding feast at
Cana to perform His first miracle and to begin His public ministry. The *Catholic Catechism* reminds us that, "The Church
attaches great importance to Jesus' presence at the wedding at
Cana. She sees in it the confirmation of the goodness of marriage and the proclamation that thenceforth marriage will be an
efficacious sign of Christ's presence."

We are the "Domestic Church."

Christ Himself said of marriage, *"For this reason a man
shall leave his father and mother and cling to his wife, and
the two shall become as one. . . . Therefore, let no man separate what God has joined. . . . Whoever divorces his wife (lewd
conduct is a separate case) and marries another commits adultery"* (*Mark* 10:7-12).

Not a lot of room for "bailing out" here! But the good news
is that God knows our weaknesses and promises help.

"From a valid marriage arises *a bond* between the spouses
which by its very nature is perpetual and exclusive; further-
more, in a Christian marriage the spouses are strengthened and,

as it were, consecrated for the duties and dignity of their state *by a special sacrament*" (*Catholic Catechism*, p. 409, #1638).

In other words, we're not in this alone.

Growing statistics reveal an American culture that has abandoned its reverence for Matrimony and the sacredness of what was once a lifetime vow. The result is one in three marriages that fail.

Divorce is devastating, but even more so to the children involved, who experience their own loss, sense of grief, and shattered dreams.

"The number one fear of young children, perhaps unspoken but nonetheless real, is the possibility that their parents would divorce" so say a growing number of psychologists and child development experts who have written and spoken on the destructiveness of divorce.

"You guys can't ever divorce, rrright?" my son Dominic once innocently asked at the supper table, after hearing of a classmate's sadness over his parents' painful divorce.

"That's right, Dominic. We're a team. But we have to remember that sometimes even good parents have problems. God says He will help us and that He is a part of our marriage. But we have to remember to pray and stay close to Him."

"That's why Christians begin their married lives in Church and the bride and groom invite their friends and family to be with them and to pray for them so that they will always have the grace to overcome any trouble or trials that come along."

Dominic, like most children growing up in an age of "no-fault" and easy divorce, simply sought reassurance.

As for Tim and Tina, who thankfully share a deep faith, similar beliefs and many common interests, they too will discover—as all married couples do—their own unique differences and maybe a few "surprises" along the way. Like who is the better grocery shopper and who has more patience with a novice teen behind the wheel (never mind my Italian temperament).

"The differences are what keeps life interesting!" my mom always says.

To be sure, there is always some risk of real disharmony and dissension. After all, we live in a fallen world and it is the prince of lies who wants discord not Christ, the Prince of Peace.

That's where prayer and staying close to the Church is crucial and makes even the big hurdles seem conquerable.

The *Catholic Catechism* devotes no less than 15 pages to the Sacrament of Matrimony and even concedes: "It can seem difficult, even impossible, to bind oneself for life to another human being." Yet it reminds us throughout of the "grace that is intended to perfect the couple's love and to strengthen their indissoluble unity. . . . By this grace they "help one another to attain holiness in their married life and in welcoming and educating their children." In fact, it says that "**Christ Himself is the source of this grace**" and "sanctifies them on the way to eternal life" (p. 409, #1641).

How's that for help?

I don't know what "surprises" Tim and Tina will discover. Perhaps Tim won't follow in his father's footsteps when it comes to grocery shopping and stretching a budget beyond even an accountant's wildest wishes. But then again, maybe he will be another chip off the old block.

One thing I know for sure, with God as their Third Partner they can't fail. All they need to do is remember to pray and ask His help.

"Love is patient; love is kind. Love is not jealous it does not put on airs, it is not snobbish. Love is never rude, it is not self-seeking, it is not prone to anger; neither does it brood over injuries. Love does not rejoice in what is wrong but rejoices with the truth. There is no limit to love's forebearance, to its trust, its hope, its power to endure. Love never fails. Prophecies will cease, tongues will be silent, knowledge will pass away . . . .There are in the end three things that last; faith, hope, and love, and the greatest of these is love" (*1 Corinthians* 13:4-8,13).

Aunt Joanie's Potatoes Au Gratin
Tim's favorite

Kids loved it

1 lb Frozen Hash Brown Potatoes
1/4 Cup Butter melted
1 Can Cream of Chicken Soup
5 oz Sharp Cheddar Cheese—grated
1/2 Cup Sour Cream
1/2 med. Onion, chopped
1/2 tsp Salt
1 1/2 Corn Flakes—crushed

Mix and put in greased pan (8 x 8). For a topping, melt 1/4 cup butter, add to 1 1/2 cup crushed corn flakes. Spoon over potatoes. Bake at 350° for about 1 hour (cover for part of the time).

* Needless to say, I double or triple this recipe.

CHAPTER 29

Good Priests From Good Families

"Called to consecrate themselves with undivided heart to the Lord and to 'the affairs of the Lord,' they give themselves entirely to God and to men" (*Catholic Catechism* on Holy Orders p. 395, #1579).

"I'm not interested in girls because I'm going to be a priest," my son, Joseph, blurted out one day in response to the playful teasing of his brothers and sisters. Exciting words to this Catholic mom, except that it comes from the mouth of a seven year old.

"What makes you think you want to be a priest?" I asked in surprise.

"Well, I dunno. I just do. I want to be like Father Burns and Joseph Johnson (a Seminarian recently assigned to our local parish). But, can I still play baseball?"

"Yes, Joseph, you can still play ball, ride a bike, and do all the things you enjoy. Look at Father Mark, the new priest at St. Charles. You saw him ride by on his bike the other day. He was with another priest friend and they were enjoying their day off together."

"Just checking it out," Joseph said.

"Time will tell if this is what God has planned for you, Joseph. There is plenty of time. Meanwhile, Dad and I will be praying for you and for all our kids because we know He has a special job for each of you."

"Remember too, priests are *called* by God. And with prayer and grace, they will respond."

The discussion with my youngest son, Joseph, got me thinking. What brought on the sudden interest and openness to the idea of a religious vocation? With no prompting on our part, we've seen the difference in our own household of kids.

What's changed?

In this mom's view, the answer is simple: seeds of interest were planted.

It *first* began subtly, with the simple and repeated act of going to Mass with the family, and knowing several priests on a personal basis.

One of those priests was Father Burns, a young associate who has a special zeal for fostering the concept of religious vocations.

Whether it's from the pulpit or in casual conversation with parishioners, Father talks *enthusiastically* about the priesthood. Here was a young, happy, joyful priest, who is obviously in love with his vocation.

Enthusiasm caused curiosity.

Secondly, Father began making frequent visits to the parish school. He hosted tours of the Church and sanctuary, including a peek in the Confessional; giving explanations of everything from the choices in Scripture readings for Sunday, to the change in vestment colors. As the youngsters became familiar with the tabernacle, chalice and sacred vessels, the rituals and meaning of the Mass and sacraments came alive.

Likewise, visits to several local religious communities of sisters were sponsored by our parish.

Another seed is planted.

Thirdly, came an emphasis on the need to *pray daily* for those in the seminary, along with an assignment for all grade schoolers.

"Today Father Burns came into our room with a big picture poster of all the men studying to be priests in our diocese," Michael, 11, announced at the dinner table.

"He came to our room too!" echoed Kari, 13; Dominic, 9; and Joseph, 7.

"We each have a seminarian to pray for this year," Michael began.

"Yeah, I have one too," the same three chimed.

"My guy is Michael Becker," Dominic offered.

"Mine is Jesse Abbott," Joseph added.

Michael and Kari, our eighth grader, boasted of their own seminarians.

A simple assignment, yet it kept each child, from Fall to June, focused in prayer on their own seminary candidate. It also reminded them that priests the young and the not-so-young need our prayers.

At our house, a nightly ritual began of mentioning the names of the assigned candidates, as well as, our own faithful priests during family prayers. A wonderful way to pray for religious vocations.

Another seed.

Fourth, the "Called by Name" vocations program sponsored by the Archdiocese was implemented in our parish. The response was positive for those attending, but more importantly, for those of us in the pews.

Here's how the "Called by Name" program works:

Parishioners were asked to call the rectory or send in names of any single women and men thought to possibly have a religious vocation. Invitations were then sent out for all to attend a dinner, relaxed and informational, with the Archbishop.

The program reminded us anew that truly God does call His shepherds by name and we must pray that the empty noise of the world does not drown out that call.

Fifth, our parish priests hosted an outdoor barbecue for vocations, inviting anyone (sixth grade level to adult) who was interested in knowing more about life as a religious. Also present were representatives from a variety of religious orders of sisters, Christian brothers, missionary, and diocesan priests and deacons, and even the Archbishop.

For many of these orders, being invited to such an event by

a local parish, and having the opportunity in a casual setting to tell about the specific focus of their ministry, was an entirely new experience.

With 80 attending (including several from this household), the evening was a tremendous success, and promises to be an annual event.

Another seed planted.

Last and most important, is daily prayer for vocations. A year ago our pastor, Father Francis Kittock, added a simple prayer to be said before all daily and Sunday Masses.

Simple seeds that inspire prayer by many and a response by some.

The late Bishop Fulton Sheen, author, lecturer, and well known TV personality, had a special zeal for priestly vocations. On many occasions he reminded his audience to "pray for priests and for vocations to the priesthood."

Paraphrasing Bishop Sheen, he said, "Satan is more interested in bringing down one priest than in winning a thousand other sinful souls who will probably merit eternal hell on their own."

"Why? Because Satan knows, perhaps more than we do, about the power of the priesthood to act as Christ's representative on earth."

The *Catechism* reminds us, "It began first with the apostles who were 'endowed by Christ with a special outpouring of the Holy Spirit.' Later, by the 'imposition of hands,' they passed on to their auxiliaries the gift of the Spirit, which is transmitted down to our day through episcopal consecration" (p. 389, #1556).

Think of it. An unbroken line of leadership from Peter, the first pope, to our present Holy Father!

"Through the sacrament of Holy Orders priests share in the universal dimensions of the mission that Christ entrusted to the apostles. The spiritual gift they have received in ordination prepares them, not for a limited and restricted mission, 'but for the fullest, in fact the universal mission of salvation to the end of the earth' " (*CCC* p. 391, #1565).

An awesome vocation, yet Christ often calls the most ordinary of men, beginning with his first hand-picked fishermen, tent makers, and tax collectors.

"Who would ever think that a kid from the inner city of Detroit would end up in a Franciscan Seminary?" one young man confided. "It was an invitation by Mother Angelica on her EWTN network that compelled me to write for more information. It took one visit to the seminary to realize this is where I belonged. I'm happy and at peace for the first time."

Father Burns talks too about the "peace" that came once his decision to enter the seminary was made. "Priesthood was always tucked away in the back of my mind. But for the most part, I felt unworthy, so I headed for life in the business world as an accountant. I began to pray to the Blessed Mother Mary, and really she gets the credit for helping me take the step to enter the seminary. When I did, a big weight lifted and a peacefulness came."

Another priest, Father Mark Huberty, told of his own journey: "I was in college seeking a degree in business, with no thought of becoming a priest. My interest began first with curiosity. I wanted some answers to give my non-Catholic roommates who had so many misunderstandings about our beliefs. I started talking to a local priest off-campus. It seemed that the more I knew, the more I wanted to know, not just for the others anymore, but for me.

"I began going to Mass more frequently and soon my love for the Eucharist couldn't be ignored. I was hooked. A degree in business or life on the outside fell by the wayside. I wanted to be a priest!"

Not to be dismissed is the fact that this young priest was raised in a loving Catholic family, with a deep reverence for the faith and priesthood.

Yet, his vocational call could have been stifled had there been no priestly mentor who patiently responded to his questions.

And then there were those antagonistic roommates.

Thank heavens!

There is a saying that goes, "Good families, good priests. One comes from the other."

With the dramatic increase in divorce and decline in church attendance, it is little wonder that family life, as well as vocations, have taken a nose dive in the past several decades.

The answer is prayer. Next, pastors and parish schools might try planting their own "seeds" in helping to promote religious vocations.

My own children discovered when attending the parish "vocations barbecue" just how "down to earth," "happy" and fun-loving the sisters and Christian brothers were.

"Most of the sisters we met were so young!" our Kari remarked. "And, they seemed so happy and excited about what they were doing with their lives."

A witness far better than any brochure or speech!

Parents, too, by their attitude and example, can help to encourage an openness to a religious call in their children. We can:

• Speak positively and prayerfully of the call to priesthood or life as a deacon, Christian brother, or sister.

• Pray for vocations and for those who now selflessly serve. They are human and not without temptation. They need our prayers.

• Encourage our children to look into a variety of religious communities and to know more about their founders the Saints through good reading material. Even if they do not have a religious vocation, they will have a greater understanding of the faith and those called by God to religious life.

• Let our children know that the priesthood is different from other vocations or careers and that while every Baptized Christian has a mission designed by God to fulfill it is only the Sacrament of Holy Orders, "through which the mission entrusted by Christ to his apostles continues to be exercised in the Church until the end of time" (*Catholic Catechism* p. 383, #1536).

It is *this* Sacrament which "permits the exercise of a *sacred power* which can come only from Christ himself through his

Church" (*CCC* #1538).

In the "ordained minister, it is Christ Himself, who is present to His Church as Head of His Body, Shepherd of His flock, High Priest of the redemptive sacrifice, Teacher of Truth. This is what the Church means by saying that the priest, by virtue of the sacrament of Holy Orders, *acts in personna Christi Capitis*" (p. 387, #1548).

"Acting in the person of Christ and proclaiming his mystery, priests are now consecrated to "preach the gospel and shepherd the faithful as well as to celebrate divine worship" (*Catholic Catechism* p. 391, #1564).

For this reason alone, priests and those in the seminary need our continued prayers. In fact, some of the most well known saints, such as St. Therese of Lisieux, St. John Vianney, and St. Alphonsus Liguori (Patron of Vocations), devoted their prayer intentions and sufferings specifically for the priesthood.

In a very real sense, we want our children to see their own vocation, whatever that may be, as a fulfillment of God's plan for them, and as the avenue not to fame and wealth but better still to eternal happiness in Heaven.

I don't know if Joseph, or any of our other children, will have a religious vocation. Time will tell. I do know that they all have been introduced to the idea thanks to the efforts of our parish priests and Bishop.

The seeds have been planted. The rest is up to prayer and God's *call*!

"Every high priest is taken from among men and made their representative before God, to offer gifts and sacrifices for sins. He is able to deal patiently with erring sinners, for he himself is beset by weakness and so must make sin offerings for himself as well as for the people. One does not take this honor on his own initiative, but only when called by God as Aaron was" (*Hebrews* 5:1-4).

Just Plain Meatloaf

1 1/2 lb. Ground Beef
1 Cup Cracker or Bread Crumbs (or you can substitute with
    oatmeal)
2 Eggs, beaten
1 8 oz can (1 Cup) Tomato Sauce
1 Onion, chopped
2 Tbsp Green Pepper
1 Salt
1 Bay Leaf, crushed
Dash Thyme
Dash Marjoram
Ketchup for Topping

Combine all ingredients but ketchup. Shape mixture in loaf baking pan. Bake at 350° about 1 hour. Just before it's done, smear top with ketchup and put back in oven. Let stand for a few minutes before serving. Serves 6 to 8. Needless to say I normally double this recipe.

* Don't be afraid to try the oatmeal and topping of ketchup. The kids love the top!

CHAPTER 30

Why Visit, If Grandpa Doesn't Know We're There?

"There is an appointed time for everything, and a time for every affair under the heavens. A time to be born, and a time to die;. . . a time to weep and a time to laugh . . . a time to mourn and a time to dance. . . a time to embrace and a time to be far from embraces, . . . a time to seek, and a time to lose" (Ecclesiastes 3:1-6).

"I don't understand why we have to visit so often," Dominic, then nine, said pleadingly. "It's not like Grandpa will know the difference. Sometimes he talks to us sometimes he doesn't. Most of the time, he doesn't even know we're there!"

"That may be true, Dommie, but we go because we love Grandpa and we want him to *always* feel loved. More importantly, we want to know that we were *always* loving to him even when he may not have been aware.

"It's kind of like when Mom and Dad go into your bedroom late at night to check on you," I explained. "We see that the windows are closed from the cold, kiss you on the cheek even though you are asleep, and tuck you in warmly if your covers have fallen. You don't know we're there, but isn't it nice to have someone watching over you?"

"Yeah, I never thought of it that way!" Dominic responded. "Just hearing our voices, seeing our faces even when he can't respond is reassuring and comforting to Grandpa. Our very presence is a reminder 'There's someone here who cares a great deal about me.' "

"But what do we talk about?" Dominic asked.

"Tell him that you're taking trumpet lessons for the first time and how excited you are. Tell him about the two home runs you helped bring in last week at your Little League game. Better yet, remind him of the times you shared a bowl of ice cream after dinner or the fun you had visiting his farm. He'd love nothing more than to have someone help him remember those good times."

"It was easy visiting Grandpa when he was in his wheel chair and we could wheel him into the day room and watch a game together or show him some photos of what we'd been doing," Michael, our 11 year-old piped in. "I liked it when he could still come home for holidays and birthdays. But now he's in bed all the time and keeps falling asleep. It's hard to know what to say. I don't think he even hears us."

"Yeah," said five year-old Joseph. "Wouldn't he just rather rest and not have us come?"

"No, Joseph, he wouldn't. And we wouldn't want that either. We have to remember that just because his eyes are closed, or he doesn't respond to what we say, doesn't mean he can't hear and understand every single thing that's being said. That's why it is so important to talk to Grandpa and to tell him things that he would like to hear about and to let him know we love him."

"Ya mean maybe he's saving his strength to get better?" Joseph asked.

"That's possible, Joseph. Or, he might not get better. He could become weaker still. What we know for sure is that this is the time for us to do the talking while he is quiet and listens. And, it's nice to talk about things that he remembers."

"Like last week," Michael said edging in. "Remember how he seemed so 'out of it,' until we started talking about Shadow, his crazy run-away horse, and a big smile came across his face?"

"That's what I mean," I said.

"Remember too," I reminded my children, "each time we visit someone who is shut-in or sick, and we do it for the love of God, it becomes a 'Corporal Work of Mercy' and we receive a *special* grace. You see, God is just never outdone in generosity!" (This is found in *Matthew* 25:34-40.)

And so began one of several discussions with several of our children about visiting loved ones who are shut-in, hospitalized, or in nursing homes.

We talked about the importance of bringing something cheerful and bright. A card, a child's drawing, a colorful picture or poster, a small plant or flower are a few items that can bring on a grateful smile and help decorate a room that could otherwise appear gloomy or "sterile."

All of this can seem distant and remote until it hits a close family member or loved one. In our case, it was my father who incurred repeated hospitalizations, and eventually went into a nursing home. Health care decisions regarding the possibility of future illness and death could no longer be ignored.

Virginia, a close family friend, and an experienced health care provider for nursing home residents and the elderly, offered the most supportive and practical advice during this difficult time.

"Some patients," she said, "only see loved ones at holidays and birthdays. It's so sad. On the other hand, you *don't* have to visit every day."

More than for Dad's sake, our visits, especially with our children, helped ease us into each stage of Dad's illness and his eventual going home to God in his death.

"In my Father's house are many mansions; if it were not so I would have told you. I go to prepare a place for you" (*John* 14:2).

Over a three-year period, Dad was hospitalized six times and was a resident in three different nursing home facilities. Each one varied greatly in atmosphere, privacy, and the care given. Yet, with each, there were things we could do to bring reminders of home and love to him.

We loaded Dad's room with an array of our childrens' hand-drawn "art"; a wallboard of family photos; as well as, mementos of good times past.

Something as simple as a clean shirt, fresh hanky, his trusted watch, a wallet with a few dollars to look over and finger, or a good shave and haircut helped maintain Dad's dignity and a degree of independence.

For women residents, Virginia tells families, "A dime store necklace and earrings, a colorful broach, or a pretty scarf, can be so uplifting. Keep it inexpensive because unfortunately, there is the possibility of things being stolen. Most importantly, let them have their purse (take out the valuables). To many women, this is a prized possession!"

As Dad's health failed, so too did his response to the items we had brought him on our visits. They then became *our own* cherished reminders.

In the end, Dad suffered from Alzheimer's disease, severe dementia, and eventually a stubborn pneumonia which filled his lungs. He became coma-like in appearance, demonstrating little if any response to our comings and goings, as his body, with feeding tubes and intravenous medications, struggled to fight back. He was in a losing battle.

Our family visits were no longer filled with cheerful conversations, but a recitation of who we were and our verbal expressions of affection. Dad showed little, if any, response.

It seemed more appropriate then, to simply gather around his bed and lift our voices in prayer and song. Christmas tunes or some of his old favorites such as "You Are My Sunshine," "Let Me Call You Sweetheart," and "I'm Looking Over A Four Leaf Clover," we hoped would lovingly prod his memory of times past.

My most startling lesson on care giving and the importance of visiting and conversing even with the chronically ill who we may *think* are unaware came just days before Dad's death.

As I sat alone by his hospital bedside one evening, watching the rhythmic breathing of his now frail chest, I leaned near his ear and began a light-hearted chatter of some of my own childhood memories: our trips to the store when he sat me on the front seat of his car next to him and sang songs (off key) to me; the time he took off work in the middle of a busy day to take me for my drivers test, hoping it would "put an end to my nagging" and I flunked the test; or his continual ribbing about my being a "lousy Italian" because I couldn't stand to eat his homemade hot peppers and spicy Italian sausage (things I now crave!).

Dad lay motionless, except for the forced breathing, as I continued my litany of "little girl memories," until I jokingly said, "You know, you are really just a crusty old Italian . . . one of those kind of guys who could never show affection. I know you love me, Dad, but would it have been so terrible to once or twice *tell me?*"

With that, Dad lifted his head off the mound of bed pillows, hoses hanging from his arms and nose, and opened his eyes. Looking down at me with lips dry and parched, he tenderly said, "You always knew I loved you!"

Music to my ears and well worth the wait!

Dad lived for nearly two weeks after that, but those were his last words to me. I learned, a valuable lesson: *Never assume* a patient is unaware!

Do you have a friend, neighbor, or loved one who would welcome your visit? Don't delay. Do it now. You will be so glad you did.

Here are a few other suggestions that we learned along the way:

• Make visits frequent but brief—15 to 30 minutes is adequate. Anything longer may be too taxing and tiring. (You do not have to visit *every* day.)

• If you are a close family member, talk openly about the kinds of medical care and the measures the patient would wish you to express on his or her behalf, should it become necessary. Assurance that someone is looking after our physical well being, as well as property and possessions, is crucial to one who becomes incapacitated.

• Attend "Care Conferences." Immediate family members are to be included in these conferences. Your insight and input is valuable. Don't be afraid to ask questions or to express concerns regarding the patient's progress or care.

• Keep conversation light and positive, as well as up-to-date about family happenings. Talk about what is of interest to the patient. Discussions focused on catastrophic illness or headlined, non-essential news can be depressing and disheartening.

• *Never* talk as if the patient is **not** part of the conversation. Even those who are unresponsive or appear incognizant, may be fully aware of what is being talked about.

• What to bring: yourself, your love, your memories! In addition: a simple greeting card, a picture or colorful poster for the wall, some photos that may trigger a fond memory, a plant or flowers (always appreciated), or a favorite food or drink if permissible.

• Tokens of loving memories—more meaningful than something new are the items seen and used throughout the years. Make sure your loved one has their personal prayer book, Rosary, book mark, Holy cards, wrist watch, a special sweater, tie, or jacket, as well as, the purse or wallet most often used. (Never mind what shape it's in!)

• Make a photo collage for the wall or "family scrapbook" of special events of the past—such as weddings, picnics, holidays. Photos can be mounted on a simple cork board. Be sure to label each one, such as, "1996 Christmas Eve with your son, Jim & his wife, Joanne and their kids, Mark, Susie and Mary." This is uplifting to the patient. It is also helpful to the care givers who, seeing the snapshots, can more easily converse about some of the people and places familiar to the patient.

• Have on hand a large calendar, perhaps marking special days or upcoming events, i.e., "Thanksgiving with family at Jim's." You may want to mark your visits to let the patient know when you will be coming next. It also helps maintain a sense of time.

• Appearance means everything! If you are a family member, make sure the patient has comfortable and clean clothing, as well as some little "extras," such as, jewelry, a pretty scarf or vest—things that are cheerful and bright. For men, a good haircut and close shave are as important as a fresh hairdo and manicured nails are to women.

• Offer a little prayer. Most patients welcome an invitation to pray. The words especially with those they know and love are familiar and comforting.

• During visits to nursing home facilities, take a moment to greet other residents. Some individuals see little of family or friends. A kind word or a few minutes of neighborly conversation can mean so much to those who are ill and shut in. For some long term residents, loneliness is the greatest affliction of all.

• Also comforting to remember: *"And God shall wipe away every tear from their eyes; and there shall be no more death, neither sorrow, nor crying, neither shall there be any more pain: for the former things are passed away"* (*Revelation* 21:4).

* Recommended reading:
The 36-Hour Day, Nancy Mac, M.A. and Peter V. Rabins, M.D., M.P.H.
A Survival Guide for Family Caregivers, Jo Horne.

"At the father's death, he will seem not dead, since he leaves after him one like himself, Whom he looks upon through life with joy, and even in death without regret" (*Sirach* 30:4-5).

Grandma Delmonico's Italian Salad

1/4 Cup Vinegar
2 Tbsp Water
2 Tbsp Sugar
Salt and Pepper to taste
Oil Olive or Mazolla Oil
Lettuce—preferrably a mixture of Romaine, Leaf, Endive
Onions (sliced thinly—ring shaped) or Green or Red Onions
Cucumbers (sliced thin)
Tomatoes, quartered in bite size pieces

Wash lettuce. Arrange in large bowl with onions. Chill. Generously pour salad oil over lettuce, cucumber, and onion mixture and chill again in frig.

Mix vinegar, water and sugar in small bowl or cup. Taste with your finger (oops—don't tell!) until you feel it is sweet enough. Pour over lettuce mixture right before dinner. Be sure to generously salt and pepper, then thoroughly mix the salad. Add tomatoes and serve.

* This and bread was a dinnertime staple in the Italian household I grew up in.

CHAPTER 31

Memories Are Made Of This

"Through Him the whole body grows, and with the proper functioning of the members joined firmly together by each supporting ligament, builds itself up in love" (*Ephesians* 4:16).

If you polled every member of your family, asking them to, "Describe a Christmas most remembered" each would probably come up with a different Christmas and a different memory. Try it! Sharing memories is more than nostalgic. It is fun, healthy, and a good way to pass on some cute stories of "remember when" to younger family members. As the old '50s tune suggests, "Memories Are Made Of This."

Of course, each of us can recall a holiday that was not so happy or joyful. As Christians we know there will be *no* perfect season or celebration until we are one with Christ in Heaven. Until then, there will be degrees of disappointment. Yet, the sharing of good times past does help fade painful memories and imperfections.

In fact, some of those imperfections can offer their own source of laughter and fun.

For instance, all of our kids like to recall the time Tim, then an incorrigible seven-year-old, got up in the middle of the night, unwrapped all the Christmas presents and put them all away in the basement after unpacking and playing with each one. Before returning to bed, he finished off the evening by eating *every* piece of candy Santa had carefully stuffed in the once hung stockings.

We awoke on Christmas morn to a living room that looked as if it had been systematically ransacked: boxes and packages were strewn everywhere or tossed in a heap under the tree.

The wailing soon began and took on a new meaning as Chrissy and Tina found their new dolls face down in the bottom of the toy chest and Tony's new trucks were neatly shelved in the basement play area.

Our clue was an unperturbed Tim, who lay fast asleep in his bed. But not for long!

Needless to say, Tim, now grown, rarely gets through a Christmas without *someone* recalling that long-ago Christmas. Thankfully, time and love offered just the space and sense of humor needed. We all enjoy recalling the year our "Midnight Prowler" stole Christmas.

There were other years and other mischievous kids, with a few marked occasions when Santa felt compelled to leave a *potato* in a kid's sock rather than the usual "stocking full of goodies."

Oh, there were still plenty of gifts but it was that lump of raw potato in the bottom of the sock that taught the lesson.

"It only happened to me once," chuckled one now-grown son, "and that was enough. I shaped up. I wasn't going to let that happen again!"

As parents, we began wiring the tree to the wall and ceiling after we learned our own lesson about a young and frisky crew. One new crawler had pulled down the entire tree, decorations and all, three times in a week. Lesson learned!

And then there was the year that our adopted son, Charlie, was chosen to be one of the angels for the school Christmas Pageant. Dressed in white from head to toe, similar to all the other angels, Charlie worried we wouldn't be able to see him.

"Now don't forget to look for me," he said. "I'll be the one in the top row toward the back."

Being the *only* dark-skinned angel on stage, we assured him we'd have no trouble spotting him!

Theresa's favorite memory was the Christmas morning she

found a beautiful (second-hand) guitar *just for her* under the tree. Even at the sceptical age of thirteen, Theresa knew there was something special about Christmas. She never knew the instrument came from a friend who heard of her wish.

Advent took on a deeper meaning the year Mary Elizabeth, then eight, came home from school and told us how we could all become "Advent Angels" by exchanging names and using the weeks before Christmas to do "little acts of kindness" anonymously for the person whose name was drawn. The kindnesses might include straightening a room, doing their chores (dishes, dusting, taking out the trash, etc.) or leaving little prayer notes with a little piece of candy under their pillow.

Of course, there are always a few rolled eyes; sighs of "Not her"; or "Oh no, he's such a nerd!" as they unwrapped the names and realize they are committed to four weeks of pampering a sister or brother who normally drove them up the wall. But that's part of the fun!

It's been a wonderful way to get our youngsters to think of others especially during this season of "I wants."

The first year Charlie moved away to college, he called home at Advent and asked if we'd picked names. When we assured him it was Advent-as-usual, he responded, "Gee, I feel left out this year."

Our eldest daughter Chrissy's favorite Christmas memory will always be the year she broke her leg in a skiing accident. The memory didn't center on the hospitalization, the surgery, or the awkwardness and immobility of the crutches.

No, it was the beautiful Christmas Eve Mass and the surprise her boyfriend, Andy, had been planning. He used the occasion, in spite of the crutches, to propose and give Chrissy an engagement ring.

As for our own "most memorable" Christmas, I think my husband John and I would always choose the Christmas long ago that drained us emotionally, physically, and financially, yet became one of the most exhilarating of all. It was the Christmas our first two adopted children arrived.

Our long awaited Tina (19 months), came from the Philippines. Five days later, Tony (2 months) the son we had recently petitioned to adopt, thinking it would take another year arrived under a special emergency medical visa from an orphanage in Vietnam.

Both were delivered to the Minneapolis/St. Paul Airport. They were so small and precious and arrived with special medical and/or emotional "needs." And we, their new mom and dad, were feeling grateful and *so* inadequate!

Walking through the airport that Christmas, with our family of two "tummy kids" Chrissy (4) and Timmy (2 1/2), along with our new daughter, Tina, and son, Tony, we could hear the Christmas carolers singing the beautiful and familiar tunes we knew and loved.

Somehow the carols seemed to settle our unsettled stomachs and remind us of the sacred season and the Christ Child's own fragile and *unplanned* delivery. God would surely watch over us and calm our fears. And so He did!

There has never been a trip to the airport, or the sound of Christmas carolers, when we don't recall that Christmas and the two blessings who were flown to us that year!

I'm always a bit troubled by those who suggest that the commercialization of Christmas *takes away* from its meaning. Only if we allow it! On the contrary, we should be overjoyed! After all, there is no other holiday, religious or secular, that is welcomed and celebrated by even the non-religious, the way that the birth of Christ is recognized.

And for those fallen away from the faith or the "secular Scrooges" amongst us, this very "commercialization" may just be that gentle and irresistible nudge that brings them to Christ.

I remember one acquaintance who smugly confided, "Christmas has gotten so commercialized, we refuse to be part of it. We really don't do much."

Hmmm.

Guess who's happy with a negative decision like that? Not God!

It will be our witness, our cheerfulness, our obvious love for

Christ and one another that offers the best reflection for those on the outside looking in.

All the more reason then, however you choose to celebrate Christmas, to take time if you can perhaps as you sit around the dinner table and share some of your own fun-loving and "memorable" stories of Christmases past.

No one can commercialize that!

"You are the light of the world. A city set on a hill cannot be hidden. Men do not light a lamp and then put it under a bushel basket. They set it on a stand where it gives light to all in the house. In the same way, your light must shine before men so that they may see goodness in your acts and give praise to your Heavenly Father" (*Matthew* 5:14-16).

Auntie Rita's Almond Snack (No Bake)
A favorite Kuharski Christmas treat

1 lb. White Almond Bark
1 1/2 Cups Spanish Peanuts
2 1/2 - 3 Cups Thin Pretzels, broken in half

Melt Almond Bark in double broiler. Break pretzels and mix with peanuts in large bowl. Pour melted bark over and mix with spatula or wooden spoon.

Spread on cookie sheet lined with wax paper. Cool. Break into pieces and store (*or hide in your bedroom closet like I do*).

CHAPTER 32

Good-bye College Freshie—Hello Empty Bed And Tidy Room—Yuk!

"The Lord is your guardian; the Lord is your shade; He is beside you at your right hand. The sun shall not harm you by day, nor the moon by night. The Lord will guard you from all evil; He will guard your life. The Lord will guard your coming and your going, both now and forever" (*Psalm* 121:5-8).

You'd think I'd get used to it by now, but I never do and probably *never* will.

We said good-bye to another who "left the nest." Each time it happens, my heart skips a beat and my head needs time for readjustment.

Our daughter, Mary Elizabeth (18), went off to college and dorm life. Prior to her going my husband, John, tried everything—tactfully urging her to stay at home and commute to a local institution.

"Mary, are you sure you don't want to stay right here where you have a nice room with your sisters and all this free food?" (Never mind the curfews, chores, family rules and rituals. And never mind that in some peoples' eyes, she's only going from small "dorm" to larger.)

After all, we're friendly and we're *family*!

But, sweet and persistent Mary had her mind set on this venture for several years, seeing it as her first step into the greater world beyond.

And that's the problem. So did Dad and I!

Perhaps, it's because as parents we know so well how cruel the world can be. In fact, the older we are the more heartless it seems with its wars, famine, abortion, prejudice, rampant crime, and our fear of those who would prey on the young and innocent.

Watching a child go off to school or the armed services is not a new experience in our household. There have been six children before Mary to leave and six more to come.

With each passing, no matter how prepared, we've experienced an invisible yet tugging ache. It's tough to "let go."

Our minds might be ready but our hearts tremble on the "what ifs." After all, **who** will remind her to "be careful"? And **who** will be there if she needs someone, as surely she will?

Worse yet, what will I do each time I pass by her bedroom? There will be no more over-flowing laundry or trash baskets, or the "casual" look of her room that often begged my occasional threat of, "either this place is picked up, or there will be a $10 fine and grounding, young lady . . . ."

Who will take over my kitchen and bake cookies because she's bored or looking for something to do?

And **who** but Mary will sense my fatigue or need and quietly appear on the scene to help with dishes, dinner, or housework?

There will be no Mary popping through my back door with her grin and dimples in full display as she brags about the $3.00 man's shirt "extra extra large" she bought at the second hand shop, or the neon nail polish she borrowed from a friend.

My Mary is gone and what bugs most of us moms when you get right down to it, is **who** will fill that void? No one can.

A nice cry always helps.

And then I pray. And pray!

Once a child leaves home it's not the same. Our protective wing can't always stretch to surround and comfort them, nor prevent hurt or harm as we once could. Now it's their wings that will be strengthened in preparation for the vocation God has planned for them.

Christian parents groom their young in preparation for God's call whatever that may be. And when they leave, we soothe ourselves with the knowledge that **we love them** and **we did the best we could**. Now they are in God's hands and we resolve to *love and parent from a distance.*

"Make no mistake," I tell my young adults. "I'm not 'letting go' completely, just because you're no longer at home."

My kids will be the first to tell you, "Mom still likes to be Mom no matter where we are or how old."

"I didn't die just because you moved away," I tell them. "I'm still around and I'm still your mother."

In today's impersonal world, our prayers and presence even if long distance should be a sign of assurance and love. Sometimes, it even brings a little laughter.

My son Charlie, who now lives in Colorado, gets a kick out of some of my phone messages, such as, "Hi Charlie, this is Mom, just calling to remind you it's so-and-so's birthday; Grandma is in the hospital; and by the way, tomorrow is a Holy Day of Obligation so don't forget to get to Mass!" (Notice the finesse of how I threw that one in?)

With our Mary's entrance into the world beyond Pahl Avenue, I'm doing the same for her that I do for the rest, *Pray* and then rely on God's word: *"Train up a child in the way he should go; and when he is old, he will not depart from it"* (*Proverbs* 22:6).

I also cling to the Blessed Mother who always hears our prayers and will plead our case. Maybe it's not so much "letting go" but "loosening the hold."

"When you pass through the water, I will be with you; in the rivers you shall not drown. When you walk through fire, you shall not be burned; the flames shall not consume you. For I am the Lord, your God, the Holy One of Israel, your savior" (*Isaiah* 43:2-3).

COMMON PRAYERS

Our Father
Our Father, Who art in heaven; hallowed by Thy name. Thy kingdom come; Thy will be done on earth as it is in Heaven. Give us this day our daily bread; and forgive us our trespasses as we forgive those who trespass against us, and lead us not into temptation but deliver us from evil. Amen.

Hail Mary
Hail Mary, full of grace, the Lord is with thee; blessed art thou among women, and blessed is the fruit of thy womb, Jesus. Holy Mary, Mother of God, pray for us sinners, now and at the hour of our death. Amen.

Glory Be to the Father
Glory be to the Father, and to the Son, and to the Holy Spirit. As it was in the beginning, is now, and ever shall be, world without end. Amen.

St. Michael the Archangel
St. Michael the Archangel, defend us in battle. Be our protection against the wickedness and snares of the devil. May God rebuke him we humbly pray, and do thou, O Prince of the Heavenly host, by the power of God, thrust into Hell Satan and all the evil spirits who prowl about the world seeking the ruin of souls. Amen.

Guardian Angel Prayer

Angel of God, my Guardian Dear, to whom God's love commits me here. Ever this day be at my side, to light and to guard, to rule and to guide. Amen.

The Memorare

Remember, O most gracious Virgin Mary, that never was it known that anyone who fled to thy protection, implored thy help, or sought thy intercession, was left unaided. Inspired with this confidence, I fly unto thee, O Virgin of virgins, my Mother. To Thee I come; before thee I stand, sinful and sorrowful. O Mother of the Word Incarnate, despise not my petitions, but in thy mercy hear and answer me. Amen.

Prayer for Vocations

O God, we earnestly beseech Thee to bless this Archdiocese with many priests, brothers, and sisters who will love Thee with their whole strength and gladly serve Thy church to make Thee known and loved.

Bless our children, bless our families. Choose from our homes those who are needed for Thy work.

Mary, Queen of the clergy, pray for us. Pray for our priests and religious and obtain for us many more.

Psalm 23

The Lord is my shepherd; I shall not want.
In verdant pastures He gives me repose;
Besides restful waters He leads me;
He refreshes my soul.
He guides me in right paths
for His name sake.
Even though I walk in the dark valley
I fear no evil; for You are at my side
With Your rod and Your staff
that give me courage (*Psalm* 23:1-4).

St Therese

St Therese the "little flower," please pick me a rose from the Heavenly garden and send it to me with a message of love. Ask God to grant the favor I implore and tell Him I will love Him daily more and more.

All for thee O Sacred Heart of Jesus.

Bibliography

New American Bible, Saint Joseph Edition, All Scripture quotations unless otherwise specified.

The Catechism of the Catholic Church, (The Catholic Catechism) United States Catholic Conference, 1994.

St. Joseph Baltimore Catechism, (Official Revised Edition), explained by Rev. Bennett Kelly, C.P. (New York, Catholic Publishing Co., n.d.).

Book of Blessings, "Blessing for Expectant Mothers," Catholic Book Publishing Company, New York, 1989.

Covenant of Love, "Apostolic Exhortation on the Family" Richard M. Hogan and John M. LeVoir, Doubleday, 1985.

The Gospel of Life, Evangelium Vitae, Encyclical Letter of His Holiness Pope John Paul II, Vatican Translation, Leaflet Missal publisher, St Paul, Minnesota, 1995.

Letter to Families, His Holiness Pope John Paul II, Vatican Translation, Editions Paulines, 1994.

The Splendor of Truth, Veritatis Splendor, Encyclical Letter of His Holiness Pope John Paul II, Vatican Translation, St Paul Books & Media, publisher, 1994.

Mother of the Redeemer, Redemptoris Mater, Encyclical Letter of His Holiness Pope John Paul II, Vatican Translation, Daughters of St. Paul, Boston, MA, 1987.

Crossing the Threshold of Hope, by His Holiness Pope John Paul II, Alfred A. Knopf, New York, 1994.

Mother Teresa, A Simple Path, Compiled by Lucinda Vardey, Ballantine Books, New York, 1995.

Raising Catholic Children, by Mary Ann Kuharski, *Our Sunday Visitor Press,* Huntington In, 1991.

Parenting With Prayer, by Mary Ann Kuharski, *Our Sunday Visitor Press,* Huntington In, 1993.

"Pope Urges Worldwide Support for Breast-feeding" *Catholic Bulletin*, Diocese of St.Paul/Minneapolis publication May 18, 1996.

"Breast-feeding's Unbiased Benefits" *Family Practice News* May 15, 1996.

"Physicians urged to advise working mothers to breast-feed" *Medical Tribune* Aug. 10, 1995.

"Developmental Risk Called High for US Children, Study raises fears they won't be responsible adults" New York Times Syn. Apr. 12, 1994.

"Panel says US raising Troubled youths, warns of implications." Mpls *Star-Tribune* Nat'l News Service, Wash. D.C. June 9, 1990.

"Valuing the Family," *Mpls Star-Tribune*, June 6, 1993.

"Family Dinners have changed but still play valued social role" Ibid, Jan. 24, 1996.

"A Meal to Share," Ibid, June 5, 1996.

Raising Positive Kids in a Negative World, Zig Ziglar, Oliver-Nelson Publishing, Nashville, 1985.

"Clean Needles, Hennepin County Needs them to fight AIDS" Mpls *Star-Tribune,* Oct. 15, 1993.

Adoption Factbook, and "Monthly Memo" Nat'l Council for Adoption, 1930 17th St. NW, Wash. DC, 20009, 1989-95. Source Dr. Bill Pierce, President.

"So Much Depends on You!" edited text of Pope John Paul II's Aug. 15 Homily at Cherry Creek State Park, *Our Sunday Visitor* Aug 29, 1993.

Lives of the Saints "For every day of the year," Rev. Hugo Hoever, S.E.Cist., Ph.D., Catholic Book Publishing, New York, 1977.

Saint of the Day Vol 2, Edited by Leonard Foley, O.F.M. St. Anthony Messenger, 1975.

"Sex Survey finds teens wish they had waited," Mpls *Star-Tribune* May 18, 1994.

INDEX

Kuharski Family Favorite Recipes

Not one of these recipes promises to be a State Fair prize winner. They are basic entrées using basic ingredients. I once took a series of gourmet cooking courses and we ate pretty fun and fancy till the kids came. While I may occasionally yearn for a stuffed pork chop I don't miss it nearly as much as I'd miss the kids!

THE
RIEHLE
FOUNDATION . . .

The Riehle Foundation is a non-profit, tax-exempt, charitable organization that exists to produce and/or distribute Catholic material to anyone, anywhere.

The Foundation is dedicated to the Mother of God and her role in the salvation of mankind. We believe that this role has not diminished in our time, but, on the contrary has become all the more apparent in this the era of Mary as recognized by Pope John Paul II, whom we strongly support.

During the past years the foundation has distributed books, films, rosaries, bibles, etc. to individuals, parishes, and organizations all over the world. Additionally, the foundation sends materials to missions and parishes in a dozen foreign countries.

Donations forwarded to The Riehle Foundation for the materials distributed provide our sole support. We appreciate your assistance, and request your prayers.

> IN THE SERVICE OF JESUS AND MARY
> All for the honor and glory of God!

The Riehle Foundation
P.O. Box 7
Milford, OH 45150-0007 USA
513-576-0032